T0350001

QUICK
VALUE

QUICK VALUE

DISCOVER YOUR VALUE AND EMPOWER YOUR BUSINESS IN THREE EASY STEPS

REED PHILLIPS

WITH CHARLES SLACK

Mc
Graw
Hill

NEW YORK   CHICAGO   SAN FRANCISCO   ATHENS   LONDON
MADRID   MEXICO CITY   MILAN   NEW DELHI
SINGAPORE   SYDNEY   TORONTO

1 2 3 4 5 6 7 8 9   LCR   26 25 24 23 22 21

ISBN   978-1-264-26964-8
MHID   1-264-26964-1

e-ISBN   978-1-264-26965-5
e-MHID   1-264-26965-X

QuickValue™ is a trademark. QuickValue is not a substitute for a formal valuation and cannot replace the professional advice of lawyers, accountants, or investment bankers regarding the value of your business in a sales process.

This publication is designed to provide accurate and authoritative information in regard to the subject matter covered. It is sold with the understanding that neither the author nor the publisher is engaged in rendering legal, accounting, securities trading, or other professional services. If legal advice or other expert assistance is required, the services of a competent professional person should be sought.

—From a Declaration of Principles Jointly Adopted
by a Committee of the American Bar Association
and a Committee of Publishers and Associations

Library of Congress Cataloging-in-Publication Data
Names: Phillips, Reed, author.
Title: Quickvalue : discover your value and empower your business in three
    easy steps : a revolutionary approach for valuing midsize companies / by
    Reed Phillips, with Charles Slack.
Description: New York : McGraw Hill, [2021] | Includes bibliographical
    references.
Identifiers: LCCN 2021023116 (print) | LCCN 2021023117 (ebook) | ISBN
    9781264269648 (hardback) | ISBN 9781264269655 (ebook)
Subjects: LCSH: Valuation. | Small—Finance.
Classification: LCC HF5681.V3 P45 2021 (print) | LCC HF5681.V3 (ebook) |
    DDC 658.15—dc23
LC record available at https://lccn.loc.gov/2021023116
LC ebook record available at https://lccn.loc.gov/2021023117

Contents

PART THREE: USING QUICKVALUE

Foreword

It's easy to assume that business owners and CEOs know everything about their companies and have all the details at their fingertips. Many work hard to create that impression, not so much out of ego as of a desire to assure everyone on board that an able pilot, who sees all, is at the controls. Yet as someone who started my first business in my twenties and has served as president and CEO of several public and private companies, all I can say is—I wish!

Owners and CEOs know a lot. They have to. They live and breathe their companies, and sincerely care about their companies' success and about the people who work there. But omniscience is for the gods. There are qualities far more valuable for any leader, such as understanding what you don't know, and what you need to know, and having the curiosity and determination to find out.

That is more challenging than it sounds. To run a company is to be bombarded daily with decisions large and small, important and mundane, critical and inconsequential. You have to be ruthless and committed to carving out time to consider big-picture questions about your mission, your strategy, and, most of all, the *value* that your company is creating.

When your company sets out to deliver best-of-class products or preeminent services, the single most effective measure of success is the value you create over time. Regardless of the industry you're in, creating value is the top job for any business leader. When a leadership team achieves value creation goals, all is right with the world. It's high fives all around. Few things are more rewarding than being part of an early-stage company that grows and matures. And when you're not creating value, even the best ideas won't amount to much. Yet because of the daily pressures and demands of running their companies, too many leaders leave value creation to chance.

What I like most about *QuickValue* is that Reed Phillips has created a simple way for owners and CEOs to stay focused on this vital idea. While just about every business manager is familiar with the concept of value drivers, this is the first time I've seen them used as foundational components in calculations to determine your company's current worth. Just as important as the number that emerges from your calculations is the actionable intelligence you will gather along the way, to help make your business stronger each year.

So don't just read this book; *use* it. Come back to it again and again and put the insights you generate into action. You won't ever get to the point where you actually know everything about your business. But that's OK: A certain degree of mystery is what keeps business—and life—interesting. What you will have is a stronger and more resilient business, one better prepared for whatever the future holds. My only gripe with Reed is that he didn't write this book sooner. When I think about my own business journey, I would have loved to have *QuickValue* by my side every step of the way.

Mike Perlis, Vice Chairman, Forbes Media LLC

Acknowledgments

This book began as a March 2020 magazine article in *Knowledge@Wharton*, the online business journal for the Wharton School of the University of Pennsylvania. My friend and colleague Jeff Pundyk, coauthor of that article, had suggested that I develop some of my ideas into "thought leadership" pieces. When Jeff suggests an idea, I listen. He was publisher of *The McKinsey Quarterly*, and as far as I'm concerned, he's got an MBA in thought leadership. Based on that article, we started to think about this book. Around that time, Jeff was recruited by Deloitte to be *its* guru of thought leadership. Thankfully, he left me in good hands by recommending business writer and author Charlie Slack, who made this book better in many ways. I could not have asked for a better collaborator. Charlie and Jeff both were influential in helping shape the ideas for the book, and for that I am grateful.

I have had the good fortune to work with excellent partners at Oaklins. My current and former partners in New York contributed suggestions and helped me formulate ideas for *QuickValue*. They include my founding partner, Roland DeSilva; current partners Jack Noble, Joanna Stone Herman, and John Kaiser; and former partners Ken Collins and Jeffrey Dearth. Ken and Jack read the manuscript and gave me helpful feedback, and both worked their magic on the figures and tables. Thanks also to Andrew Eaddy and Colton Smith for their work on figures and comparables analyses. Many other Oaklins colleagues from around the world deserve my thanks for providing helpful anecdotes. I mention them in the book. One who is not mentioned, but should be recognized, is Chris Scales, executive director of Oaklins. He is based in Barcelona and keeps our organization humming with his small but efficient team. His team, including Dan Searle and Oriol Roger Monserrat, created the Oaklins Index with public company multiples for more than 100 industries in cooperation with S&P's Capital IQ.

Others who generously contributed their time to improve the book include Dan McCarthy, Mark Leiter, and David Orth.

Thanks to my editor, Stephen Isaacs at McGraw Hill, and to my agent, Steve Harris at CSG Literary Partners. Both were immediately enthusiastic about the book and indispensable in making it happen. Thanks also to the copyediting and marketing teams at McGraw Hill and to Judith Newlin, my new editor who replaced Stephen Isaacs upon his recent retirement.

My wife, Sarah, encouraged and inspired me every day. Without her steadfast support, this project would not have happened, and she has my enduring thanks in addition to love. It helps that Sarah, too, is a book author; she has written two excellent cookbooks. This book was completed during the COVID-19 months of March 2020 through March 2021. When the pandemic began, I made three resolutions: have lunch with my wife every day, since I was working from home; walk our two dogs in Central Park every morning when they can run off-leash before 9 a.m.; and write a book. Sticking to all three resolutions helped make a dark year considerably brighter. Thanks also to my parents, Reed and Nancy; my and Sarah's four children, Tom, Alex, Liz, and Zach; and the family dogs, Duke and Coco.

And, finally, thanks to the hundreds of business owners and executives I have been privileged to work with and befriend over the past 30 years. I have been constantly amazed by their ingenuity, hard work, courage, integrity, and resourcefulness. They have taught me more than I can ever repay. If this book helps empower a single business owner to better understand the value of what she has created and move one step closer to fully realizing her dreams, it will have been more than worth the undertaking.

QUICK
VALUE

PART ONE

GETTING READY

CHAPTER 1

Why Valuation Matters

Years ago I worked with a company whose owner had received an offer of $150 million from a prospective buyer. Many entrepreneurs dream of that scenario through the long years of sweat and toil it takes to build their business. The offer was generous—10 times EBITDA (earnings before interest, taxes, depreciation, and amortization), the most commonly used measurement of profits. The company's direct competitors were selling for 6 to 8 times EBITDA.

Yet rather than sell, the owner chose to follow another entrepreneurial dream—handing the business down to the next generation. His daughter had worked for Silicon Valley technology companies and she felt sure that she knew what levers to pull to propel the business to even greater value. Over the next several years the owner and his daughter invested $10 million of profits and the lion's share of their energy into a forward-looking digital strategy. Unfortunately, while this process was under way, their core business began to decline—imperceptibly at first and then steeply. Their intense focus on the new strategy diverted their attention. They were prompting customers to migrate to digital platforms at the expense of the traditional business. Soon the core business slipped from profitability, and the digital business, which was expected to replace those profits, was underperforming. By the time we began working with them, most of their efforts were aimed at avoiding bankruptcy. It all happened so seamlessly that the owner and his daughter were taken completely by surprise.

What went wrong? In short, the family had no working knowledge of the true value of the business. From time to time, in order to obtain financing, the company had hired outside experts to conduct traditional valuations. But the owner and his daughter themselves had never looked that far under the hood. If anything, the valuation process had seemed like a nuisance or a distraction from more important matters at hand. As such, they had never taken the time to consider on their own what each business unit was worth to the overall company, nor to systematically analyze the underlying qualities—the *value drivers*—that were most essential to the company's success.

Such knowledge might have encouraged the founder to put emotions to the side, accept the offer, and use the proceeds to finance a new challenge for himself and his family. Or it might have upheld the conviction to hold onto the company and unlock new areas of value. It might have helped guide the digital strategy, telling the family how much time, effort, and cash to devote to it. And it would have alerted them to the potential decline of their core business long before that reached a crisis level. They would never have left such an important part of their business on autopilot.

With so much at stake, how could the founder and his daughter overlook such an essential tool and rely instead on guesswork and hunches? I will answer that question by posing a few others:

- If you own or run a midsize business, do you have a firm understanding of its value? Right now—at this moment?

- Do you know with certainty how much value you created in the past year?

- Can you pinpoint in your business where value is being created or where it is declining?

If so, congratulations. But more than 30 years of experience working with midsize companies tells me you are part of a small minority. Most of the hundreds of owners and CEOs I have worked with have no systematic approach to understanding what is driving the value of the companies they have spent years or a lifetime building. And they are taking a huge risk, flying just as blind as the owner of the company described above.

Why Midsize Companies?

Even the largest companies lose sight of what is driving their value; it happens more often than you might imagine. In 2001, the Walt Disney Company famously acquired the Fox Family Channel for $5.2 billion. A few years later, when the acquisition underperformed, a rigorous valuation showed the Fox Family

Channel's total worth had slipped to just $1.4 billion. As James B. Stewart describes in *DisneyWar*, Disney executives were left trying to decipher, after the fact, how nearly $4 billion in value simply disappeared.[1]

In large companies with many business lines, value declines may be lost in the rounding. At midsize companies ($10 million to $1 billion in revenue), similar missteps can be devastating. There are roughly 200,000 such companies in the United States, accounting for a third of private-sector US GDP.[2] More sophisticated than mom-and-pop outfits but less complex and unwieldy than giant corporations, they run the gamut from family-owned to sole proprietorships, partnerships, and nonprofits. They may be privately held, owned by private equity investors, or, in fewer cases, publicly listed. Their owners and executives are obsessed with day-to-day operations but have only crude benchmarks for estimating value: rough multiples and comparables, best-guess five-year plans, and the natural optimism of entrepreneurs. You see it over and over: unrealistic ideas of what a business is worth, along with a lack of tools and processes to properly assess it. It is the most common reason why good executives make bad decisions.

Valuation in the Digital Age

To properly guide your business, you need a valuation every year. Not a traditional valuation by outside experts (though those assessments have their place), but one that you and your team conduct as a way to unearth hidden value and detect problem areas while there is time to fix them. That is especially true in the digital age, when change is accelerating and competitors that you may not even be aware of are trying to knock down your door.

The biggest game changer for companies in the past decade has been the emergence and growth of powerful digital businesses such as Amazon, Apple, Facebook, and Google. They have reshaped the global economy and changed customer expectations—dramatically upsetting the applecart for legacy businesses. In this new world, nothing causes wilder and faster swings in valuation than digital disruption. Companies that appear to be performing well and maintaining their historic levels of revenue and EBITDA might be surprised to find themselves worth half of what they were just a year ago. Even valuations for businesses in "hot" sectors can change quickly and with little warning. CEOs often say they are so consumed with their digital transformation that understanding their value is a lower priority, especially if they are not considering an imminent sale. Yet only when you know what is driving the value of your business can you steer your digital transformation in the right direction.

The reason most companies overlook this essential process is that traditional valuations are complicated, time-consuming, and expensive. They require an objective third party to create them. Third-party appraisers worry that their valuations will be challenged, so they use every available valuation method to cover all bases, and they take lots of time to get there. Busy executives at midsize firms avoid these distractions like the plague. They go through the process only when they absolutely must— for example, when there is an offer on the table, or they need a loan, or a partner wants to cash out, or some other event arises that is likely to transform the company.

Beware of Valuation Substitutes

Because the process is usually reactive instead of active, owners rarely use valuation as a working part of their strategy. Instead, they rely on easier-to-arrive-at metrics such as revenue, EBITDA, year-over-year growth, number of customers, market share rankings versus competitors, and industry awards as their measurements of how they are performing and what they have achieved.

Now, those are all important measurements—but none is a substitute for a thorough valuation. Those numbers, out of context, may even give you a false sense of security or lead you to focus on the wrong areas. I am reminded of the line from the movie *Caddyshack*, when Ty Webb (Chevy Chase) tells uptight fellow golfer Judge Smails (Ted Knight) that he never keeps score. How, the judge inquires, do you measure yourself against other golfers? "By height," Ty responds. The line perfectly captures the character's and the movie's loopy irreverence. But when it comes to how your company measures up against the competition, metrics such as revenue or the number of customers you have offer no more of a complete picture than the height of PGA professional Rory McIlroy would in telling you why he had won so many golf tournaments.

Sports analogies abound because business, like sports, is all about keeping score. In baseball, if you want to know the best team in the National League, one statistic gets right to the heart of the matter—not the team batting average or on-base percentage, but how many games the team has won. The same goes for businesses: The best companies are the ones that create the most value.

Thus, valuation serves as the best prism through which to examine all the individual qualities of your business. A baseball manager considers ways to improve the team's roster, its batting average, on-base percentage, and strikeouts versus walks, all with the end goal of driving up wins versus losses. In the same way, a close analysis of your income, cash flow, and balance sheet, along with all your company's strengths and weaknesses, serves the underlying purpose of helping you create value.

At Oaklins International, one of the world's largest investment banking organizations focusing on midsize businesses, our success depends on our ability to quickly and accurately determine the value of companies we might represent for sale or those we might acquire on behalf of a client. Over the past three years, our 850 professionals in 45 countries have completed on average almost 370 M&A deals, financings, and valuations each year.

We cannot spend the time it would take to conduct a traditional valuation involving third-party experts for every one of these deals. And even if we could afford the time, we would not go that route. For all their mathematical formulas and the aura of scientific certainty, traditional valuations are often subjective and overly complex and are driven by the needs and agendas of whomever the valuation is created for.

The QuickValue method is based on the conviction that owners and executives should not have to hire third-party appraisers—whether valuation firms, accountants, or investment bankers—in order to understand their value. They should be able to create a detailed valuation with an internal team, and without financial projections. Your team already has the information it needs about your business, and it can obtain the other information through research and intelligence gathering. In addition to this book, you will find more information and resources at www.quickvaluemethod.com. QuickValue provides a faster, easier, and better method for arriving at the information you need to move your business forward. While valuation is often seen as a tool for selling a company, it can also be an essential strategy tool for making your business stronger and more competitive. This process is designed to reveal the most useful numbers and insights while eliminating the excess noise and distraction that traditional valuation generates.

The QuickValue Difference

Most traditional valuations rely on "triangulation," using a few separate methods and then finding a number that fits somewhere in the middle. Triangulation is time-consuming and expensive and often has more to do with CYA than M&A. It is necessary mainly for tax purposes or during a legal dispute—times when another party has reasons to challenge your valuation.

One traditional method, discounted cash flow (DCF), estimates value based on forecasts of a company's future financial results. I have found this to be especially problematic for mid-size companies. Most do not have good projections, if they have them at all. When they do, projections often involve applying percentage increases or decreases to revenue and expenses based on the most recent trends. What's more, a DCF-based valuation is highly dependent upon assumptions such as discount rates, terminal growth rates, and/or exit multiples; and small changes in any of these variables can swing a valuation wildly. At best, it is a haphazard and speculative approach.

QuickValue, by contrast, is the only method that uses value drivers to determine what your company is worth. Why does that matter? Because value drivers are the essential qualities that define your business—not in some imagined and hoped-for future, but right here and right now. These qualities may include your ability to withstand economic downturns, the stability of your revenue, or the barriers to entry for potential competitors. Value drivers are what make your company different from any other, including your closest competitors. Instead of pegging your value to what "average companies" in your industry are worth (as some methods do), QuickValue operates on the premise that *there are no average companies*. Value drivers enable you to unlock, understand, and capitalize on what makes you unique.

In this book, we will examine how to identify your value drivers and score each on a scale of 0 to 10. Then you will use market-rate multiples of public companies to assess the value of businesses similar to yours. In a perfect world, we would use M&A and financing multiples—results from recent transactions. Yet because these deals happen infrequently, available statistics for your industry may be a year or two old—an eternity in today's business environment. Public company financial results are usually current within three months, and the stock price is set daily. Depending on your specific industry, EBITDA multiples of public companies will usually be higher than M&A multiples. SaaS Capital, an investor in software-as-a-service (SaaS) companies, has tracked the differences for many years and has concluded that M&A multiples are 28 percent lower than public company multiples.[3] As you will see in Chapter 5, QuickValue offers a straightforward formula to account for these variations.

When traditional valuations do take market-rate multiples into account, too often they focus on a single median to determine the value of a business. This rests on the assumption that all businesses are average. But they are not. Some are worth more than others and deserve a higher multiple. Others deserve a lower multiple. QuickValue replaces the median with a range of multiples, and then uses your Value Driver Score to find where you fit in that range.

Once you have gotten comfortable with the ideas and methods outlined in this book, finding your QuickValue once a year (or even more frequently) comes down to three straightforward steps:

- **Step 1.** Identify and rate the key value drivers for your business to determine your Value Driver Score.

- **Step 2.** Compare yourself with similar businesses through a close analysis of market-rate multiples, to determine your multiples range.

- **Step 3.** Bring it all together by combining the Value Driver Score from Step 1 and the multiples from Step 2 to calculate the current value of your company.

With your recently updated valuation in hand, you will have an essential tool to guide your future. And you will have a leg up on competitors who are still letting valuation slide. This book will show you how to use your QuickValue number as an integral part of all key operations, including:

Comparing your value creation from one year to the next. Instead of relying solely on revenue and EBITDA, which are only part of the story, QuickValue will enable you to identify evolving trends in real time.

Guiding your growth strategy. Regardless of industry or history, just about every company is undergoing a digital transformation of one sort or another. A clear understanding of value will help prioritize where you invest or divest and will encourage better and more thoughtful planning.

Setting proper incentives for employees. Too often, these incentives are based on revenue or EBITDA growth. Measuring and rewarding value creation is a better way to align the performance of the management team with the objectives of the owners.

Tapping funds for growth. With an abundance of private equity money looking to invest in good companies, you will have already done much of the legwork in establishing your value before exploring financing options.

Responding decisively to an offer. If you are approached by a buyer and offered a price, you will know whether it is fair, and can make an informed decision. This last point is crucial. Too often, we see entrepreneurs selling their companies for less than they should because they do not know the true value. The buyer, usually a large company or private equity firm, may spot that value where the owner does not and optimize it once the buyer has gained control. You are the one who built the business; you, your family, and your shareholders deserve to realize the full value. At the same time, you need to recognize a good offer when you see one. Far too often, business owners hold out for a better price because of a distorted view of their company's worth, only to see the market move beneath them and their value erode.

Meet Sylvia A.

Over the course of this book, we will look at real-life examples to illustrate some key points. But it may also help to dive in on a single company to see how QuickValue can be put to use to answer the most challenging questions. Meet Sylvia A., the founder and owner of a thriving market research firm in Boston. She is a hypothetical character, but her challenges are real. She is a composite of the business leaders I have had the pleasure of working with over the years: brilliant, driven, optimistic—and yet not sure what her company is worth.

As a business school professor, Sylvia was engaged by a major company in the consumer packaged goods industry to develop a new technology based on her academic research in social listening. Sylvia soon realized she was on to something that would be attractive to other companies as well. She hired a few of her business school colleagues and launched a market research firm she called Metrics Mavens.

Eight years later, Metrics Mavens has grown into a preeminent new age market research company. Timing, as they say, is everything. Like all successful entrepreneurs, she has enjoyed good luck to go with her skills. During Metrics Mavens' gestation, market research overall has evolved from a sleepy cottage industry into one worth nearly $80 billion per year,[4] as more companies recognize the need for data and insights to understand consumer behavior.

Success has propelled Sylvia to heights she hardly imagined: a hundred employees and a sleek new headquarters downtown, headline speaking engagements around the world, appearances on prominent business television networks, and interviews published in the *Wall Street Journal* and the *New York Times*. Yet for all the success, nagging questions keep her up at night. How big can or should Metrics Mavens become? How can it stay ahead of the imitators that have sprung up out of nowhere? Where should the company go next? At a personal level, should she keep growing in the role of owner/CEO or find a buyer and return to the research she loves? But what would the company even be worth? She has never had her company formally valued—there just never seemed to be the time or need.

Then, over wine and cheese at a market research conference in Orlando, all those questions unexpectedly crystallize. Martin S., the CEO of a much larger market research firm, asks if she would consider selling.

When she hesitates, he says, "Why don't you at least tell me last year's revenue and EBITDA so I can make an offer?"

Sylvia shares that revenue was $32 million with an EBITDA of $10 million.

Martin responds evenly, "We'll pay 7.5 times EBITDA."

The number registers: 7.5 times EBITDA—$75 million! For a company that eight years ago was little more than an idea. A stray vision of that beach house on Nantucket pops into her mind. But is it the right offer? Is she even ready to sell? She thanks him and asks for two weeks to consider.

On her way to the airport for the flight back to Boston, she calls Joanna M., her CFO. They will need to work quickly—but where to begin? They have two weeks to make a decision that could alter the destiny of her company and the careers of a hundred employees, not to mention forever changing Sylvia's own life. Two weeks, and the clock is already ticking.

Over the course of this book, we will check in frequently with Sylvia and her team as they use QuickValue to get a true understanding of the company's value, weigh their options, and make the best decisions for the days ahead. Who knows—you may recognize some of Sylvia in yourself.

CHAPTER 2

Understanding Traditional Valuation

As we just read, our new friend Sylvia A. received an exciting offer for her company. Before she can respond, she needs to quickly determine how much the company is worth. Ideally, she would already have this information in hand. At some point within the past year, she and her team would have gone through the process of determining just that. A detailed knowledge of the drivers of that value could have helped her and her team make key decisions all through her eight years in business. Fortunately for Sylvia and Metrics Mavens, we are going to help her find an accurate valuation that she and her team can rely on not just to respond to the offer on the table, but to guide future decision-making should she decide not to sell.

Let's start by looking a little bit closer at how valuation has traditionally worked (or not worked) for midsize companies. If you have been through a formal valuation in the past, this may serve as a refresher. If you haven't, this background will give you a solid context for the goals and purposes of valuations so that you can better understand why and how QuickValue differs. We will also look at the other extreme—the informal "word-of-mouth" valuation process that too many business owners fall back on by default. We will consider the pitfalls and fallacies of making easy assumptions about your company's value, and how those assumptions could come back to haunt you.

Finally, we will look at what a valuation system should provide in order to become a practical, workable, and essential component of a midsize business's ongoing operations. I call these "The New Rules for Valuing Midsize Companies."

Traditional Valuation Methods

Say your company is seeking a major bank loan for capital improvements. Your bankers tell you that before they can consider your request, you are going to need a formal valuation by a professional appraiser. Through references, you find a qualified and respected candidate—most likely a certified appraiser, an accountant, or an investment banker.

The first thing that outside expert is going to do is ask you to turn over copious amounts of information about your company—including financial statements and projections as well as other reports that describe the performance of the business. Though this will likely feel invasive, there is nothing untoward about the request. Your appraiser is not part of your company and will need a lot of information in order to make informed calculations. Still, the process can be time-consuming and onerous. Over the next several weeks you and/or your financial managers are going to be peppered with requests for information on a surprisingly wide array of subjects, such as revenue by source, detailed expenses, a breakdown of general and administrative costs, patents and trademarks, business plans, growth strategies, a competitive analysis, revenue for the top 10 customers or clients, metrics used to measure performance, staffing costs, and contracts with third-party suppliers.

You may ask yourself why appraisers need all these details. The answer is that before they can even begin to assess the value of your company, appraisers need to figure out which of the many accepted valuation methods best apply to your business. They're going to do that by collecting the information needed for *every method*. Then they'll use the process of elimination to narrow the list to a final three (or, in some cases, four) methods that work best. That's a lot of numbers! Here are the five most widely used and commonly accepted approaches to traditional valuation:

1. **Book value.** Using your company's balance sheet, the appraiser subtracts liabilities from assets to get the value of the business. This method is generally the least accurate and produces the lowest value but is also the easiest. In my experience, book value is rarely used to value ongoing, successful businesses. It becomes more relevant for businesses in distress or with hard assets that are not generating much profit.

2. **Publicly traded comparables.** Here, the appraiser compiles multiples of revenue and EBITDA for companies that are similar to yours but that are publicly traded. This method is frequently used and is considered to be very accurate if you choose the right set of similar companies. However, the companies in this group are often much larger than the company you may be valuing—so special adjustments must be made to account for your smaller size and scope. (As you will learn in Chapter 5, public company comparables are an integral part of QuickValue as well. We'll discuss how to account for the size differential.)

3. **Private transaction comparables.** Your appraiser looks for multiples of M&A and financing transactions involving companies similar to yours. This method is also used frequently and is one of the most accurate, since the transactions typically involve midsize companies such as yours rather than publicly traded firms. That's assuming, of course, that you can find a sufficient number of recent transactions to analyze. One challenge of this method is that there may be only a handful among companies your size, and many of those may be outdated. Imagine pricing your house based on what your next-door neighbors sold theirs for three years ago. (Transaction comparables also play an important part in QuickValue. As with publicly traded comparables, we will examine how to account for this discrepancy.)

4. **Discounted cash flow.** Here, your appraiser estimates
    the future cash flows of the business and discounts
    those cash flows to account for risk and the time value
    of money in order to estimate the present value of the
    business. This method is heavily used by appraisers
    because they consider its premise—that future cash
    flows are the best determinate of present value—to
    be well grounded. That's because investors view the
    ability to generate cash flow as one of a business's most
    important characteristics when determining its value.
    Yet as we will see below, there are some drawbacks.

5. **Leveraged buyout.** The leveraged buyout (LBO) method
    estimates the value that buyers should place on a
    business, assuming they intend to use a combination of
    debt and equity to fund the purchase. It estimates how
    much debt can be borrowed based on the company's
    financial performance. Private equity investors
    frequently use the LBO method because their business
    model depends on using both equity and debt to
    acquire a business. LBO analysis usually gives a lower
    valuation than the comparables and DCF methods
    because its aim is to ensure that debt borrowed against
    the company can be serviced and repaid. Typically, a
    large portion, if not all, of the company's excess cash
    will be used to pay down debt.

Each of these methods has strengths and weaknesses, and
within the five are methods within methods, which can quickly

become complex. We will take a closer look at discounted cash flow, because it is so popular among appraisers.

One variety is the "cash flow perpetuity formula." If that term (for a measurement of a company's growing value over time) is not confusing enough, take a look at the formula used for it, as expressed in one of the standard valuation textbooks:[1]

$$\text{Continuing value}^T = \frac{\text{FCF}^{t+1}}{\text{WACC} - g}$$

To use this formula, you need to know that FCF^{t+1} is the normalized level of free cash flow, that WACC is the weighted average cost of capital, and that g is the expected growth rate in free cash flow in perpetuity. And that is just one among multitudes of calculations that traditional valuation methods call for.

Even simpler versions of the DCF method require financial data that may not be readily available for most midsize companies. To create the DCF model, you need at least three years of financial projections allowing you to determine how much cash the business can produce. Once the aggregate cash is calculated, it must be adjusted by a discount factor to obtain the present value of the business. When the discount rate is applied, future cash flows are converted into current dollars by taking into account the effects of inflation and the risk that the cash flows may not be achieved. A commonly used discount rate is 15 percent, which means that $1,000 in cash flow next year is worth only $870 in today's dollars ($1,000 divided by 1.15).

In theory, the DCF method is logical enough. Yet few midsize companies have the sort of fully developed financial projections to substantiate it. Most have a current-year budget, but hardly any forecast beyond that. Today, with business moving at a faster pace than ever before, companies have even less confidence in forecasting.

And even if companies do have financial projections, DCF still presents major problems. Projections are merely a company's best guess of what will happen in the future. Three-year projections can't be proved accurate until those three years have gone by and actual results are reported. Projections and actual results rarely match up, even when a company has a strong history to use as a guide. One company I worked with a few years back was growing rapidly and increasing in profitability. Projections were created at the end of 2016 that seemed realistic based on past performance. As shown in Table 2.1, three years later, when the company shared its actual results, it was apparent how far off those estimates were, particularly regarding 2019 EBITDA.

TABLE 2.1 Comparison of Income Projections Versus Actual Results

	Projections Made in 2016			Actual Results		
	2017	2018	2019	2017	2018	2019
Revenue ($ millions)	$23.9	$34.5	$41.9	$21.4	$28.3	$35.0
EBITDA ($ millions)	$9.3	$13.5	$16.5	$6.9	$6.8	$10.5

Source: Oaklins files.

It should be noted that this company produced *strong results!* Revenue grew by $13.6 million and EBITDA by $3.6 million from 2017 to 2019. However, when we compare the actual results with what was projected earlier, revenue is lower by $6.9 million and EBITDA is lower by $6 million. In other words, despite their popularity, DCF-based appraisals require accurate data based on projections that are almost always, by nature, *inaccurate.*

Other appraisal methods present different challenges. For example, an early-stage company may have low revenue and negative EBITDA, so publicly traded comparables and private transaction comparables methods based on current revenue and EBITDA might give an artificially low (or high) valuation. That is why, instead of picking one approach, most appraisers will use several valuation methods and then apply a weighting, based on relevancy, for each. The logic behind this is that all parties—whether a buyer, bank, investor, owner, or the Internal Revenue Service—will be reassured that the appraisers have made a reasonable effort to obtain a fair valuation if they can demonstrate having explored several methods.

Say, for example, an analysis of publicly traded comparables produces a value estimate of $400 million–$425 million, while a DCF analysis puts the value at $375 million–$435 million, and an LBO calculation arrives at $395 million–$450 million. Most observers will draw confidence from the fact that the three valuations are in the same ballpark. Through a process of triangulation, it is reasonable to assume a range of $400 million–$425 million for the company's actual value.

And note that while the triangulation process may get *close* to the company's value, the actual target is still a guesstimate. Think of three darts on a board, with the bull's-eye somewhere in the middle. (In the ensuing chapters, we'll see how QuickValue, rather than triangulating various valuation methods, actually integrates your calculations into a single value—in other words, with QuickValue, the results and the bull's-eye are one and the same.)

By the time the traditional valuation process is finished, a business may spend anywhere from $5,000 to $50,000, depending on how complex the valuation is, and up to four weeks. Small wonder, then, that telling a business owner or executive to produce a valuation is greeted with the same enthusiasm doctors get when advising a patient to schedule a colonoscopy. Instead of saying, "Great, let's get it done," the typical reaction, from the patient and the business owner, is, "Do I have to?" Then, procrastination sets in, and the owner waits, hoping that the need for this unpleasant task will simply go away.

Best Guesses and Word of Mouth

Unfortunately, avoiding valuations is as risky for your business as avoiding colonoscopies can be for your health. And the fact is that owners and business executives who are so methodical and rigorous about building their companies often look for shortcuts in valuing what they have created. When the subject of their company's value comes up, they may resort to the other end of the valuation scale: assumptions based on hearsay, popular wisdom, and conjecture—the corporate equivalent of urban legends.

Take, for example, a group of beverage executives gathered at an annual industry conference. During a meet-and-greet in the ballroom before dinner, the subject of business value comes up.

"In our industry, 15 times EBITDA is pretty standard for companies of all sizes," offers the CEO of a midsize soft drink company. (Hereafter, I'll use "x" in place of "times" since this denotation is commonly used by the investment banking industry.)

The six executives clustered around nod in agreement, while silently doing the math in their heads to approximate the value of their respective firms. For some if not most of those executives, that simple equation—15x EBITDA—may be enough to sustain them when they return home. Through 70-hour weeks of backbreaking labor and pivotal business decisions based on precise calculations, they take comfort in knowing or *thinking* they know what their company is worth. Who needs the pain and cost of a formal valuation?

Yet those owners are missing a key opportunity. Industrywide guesses don't reveal anything about the unique qualities of their companies. At best, 15x EBITDA might serve as a starting point for an owner trying to sell. But if a sale is still years away, it won't tell her anything about her market share, product quality, time to market, or any of the other value drivers that make her company different. Thus, it can do nothing to inform her business strategy. And besides that, numbers passed along informally may be inaccurate.

For starters, who knows where that one executive came up with 15x? Maybe an investment banker he knows gave him the average of the last 10 M&A transactions in the industry. Or maybe he found the average EBITDA multiple for public company valuations by tracking their stock values. Regardless of the source, assuming that all beverage companies, including one's own, can be valued at the same multiple is a fallacy, and potentially a dangerous one.

When I examined EBITDA multiples for 20 public companies in the beverage production industry, I found multiples ranging from a low of 10.4x to a high of 33.1x, as shown in Table 2.2. And this kind of range is typical of most industries.

Our conference attendee who cited the 15x calculation was actually quite close to the industry's *median* EBITDA multiple of 15.3x for public companies. But what does that tell us about the condition and value of any given company? Not much. It's

TABLE 2.2 EBITDA Multiples for 20 Publicly
Traded Beverage Production Companies

	EBITDA Multiple
Highest	33.1x
Median	15.3x
Lowest	10.4x

Source: PitchBook, July 2, 2020.

improbable that any, let alone all, of the companies headed by executives at that conference would command a 15.3x multiple. A top performer with steady growth and a product line favored by the right demographics might command a 20–30x multiple, while a struggling firm with an outdated product line might command just 11x, with the rest falling somewhere in between.

Let's assume one of the companies at the conference has $20 million in EBITDA. Depending on where this company falls on the spectrum of value, from highest to lowest, its value could be as high as $662 million or as low as $208 million (see Table 2.3).

TABLE 2.3 Valuations for a Beverage Production Company with $20 Million EBITDA

	EBITDA Multiple	EBITDA ($ millions)	Valuation ($ millions)	Variance vs. the Median
Highest	33.1x	$20	$662	116%
Median	15.3x	$20	$306	NA
Lowest	10.4x	$20	$208	−32%

Source: PitchBook, July 2, 2020.

If the owner of this company assumed his multiple was 15x based on what he heard at the conference, he could be off in value by as much as $362 million on the high side or $92 million on the low side. Clearly, he needs more precision when valuing his company!

Another all-too-common valuation shortcut involves fixating on a single transaction. You may believe that a company that recently sold for a certain amount is much like your own. Therefore, your own company must be worth the same. While there may, in fact, be similarities, that doesn't mean that the metrics from that transaction can be extrapolated to determine your value. That company may be larger, it may have better technology, or it may be growing faster.

One prospective client told me about a company just like hers that sold for $1 billion. My ears perked up: $1 billion is a big valuation. Now, to her credit, the owner did not assume that her own much smaller company was worth that much. Still, the comparison she used to estimate her company's value was far too simplistic. The $1 billion company had 330,000 customers. By dividing the sales price by 330,000, she figured the buyer was paying a little more than $3,000 per customer. Her own company had 70,000 customers. Multiplying 70,000 times $3,000, she figured her own company to be worth in the neighborhood of $210 million.

Unfortunately, she did not know any other key metrics of the company with which she was comparing her own. Nor had she undertaken the sort of deep, incisive look at her own business that could have given her a better basis for estimating its value. As it happened, given her company's relatively modest revenue and other factors, she might have been able to realize, at most, $50 million from a sale. Now let's be clear: That's an amazing accomplishment. Anyone who has built a company worth $50 million has beaten the odds, taken bold risks, overcome countless obstacles, proved every naysayer wrong, and achieved a level of success that most entrepreneurs could only dream of. Still, you can imagine the poor decisions that even a brilliant business leader might make—decisions affecting the future of her business, her employees, and her own life and family—by assuming that the business was worth four times more than it actually is.

Owners and business executives aren't the only ones tempted to use valuation shortcuts. Though they should know better, investment bankers do it, too. The difference is that bankers are usually well versed in valuations. They will have a good idea of the valuation ranges for the industry sectors in which they specialize. It is not usual for bankers to receive phone calls from prospective clients they have never met or talked with before. Even in this initial call, they have to be ready for the prospective client to ask what the business might be worth. Although the banker has not yet done research, he or she will be tempted to respond out of a desire to be helpful and demonstrate expertise.

The New Rules for Valuing Midsize Companies

You do not have to choose between a lengthy, multimethod valuation versus one based on hearsay and supposition. The purpose of this book is to show you that, as a midsize business, you *can* conduct straightforward and accurate valuations on a regular schedule. By doing so, you will have the power to better understand your current business, monitor your progress from year to year, and plan for the future.

Having worked with hundreds of midsize businesses over the years, I've become intimately familiar with the challenges they face. For it to be of any practical use, a valuation system must find that sweet spot between the extremes. As such, QuickValue is built around six basic principles—The New Rules for Valuing Midsize Companies—taking into account both the needs of midsize businesses and their resources:

Rule 1. Managing a business today requires a valuation at least once a year—whether or not you plan to sell. No ifs, ands, or buts. How can you make decisions about growing your business unless you know how much value you are creating or where, among all your operations, that value is being created? Without this information, you risk focusing your efforts on areas that do not add value or that add less value than other initiatives. An annual valuation is as critical as your annual budget. It is the basis of your road map to the future.

Rule 2. Your staff is capable of preparing a valuation. Putting your in-house experts on the job helps ensure an accurate valuation even as you avoid the expense of a third-party appraiser. QuickValue is easy to use, and much of the information you need is already available to your staff. They know your business better than an appraiser ever will.

Rule 3. One valuation method is plenty—if it's the right one. You do not need three methods from which to triangulate your value. Doing so is time-consuming and makes the process needlessly complex. QuickValue uses public company multiples, informed by private transactions, to arrive at a single value.

Rule 4. You can develop an accurate valuation without financial projections. I have established that you can value your business using the market multiples for public companies. QuickValue does not require financial projections, which makes the valuation process much easier. Most midsize companies do not create financial projections three to five years into the future, so this information is not readily available and would need to be created with great effort and time.

Rule 5. Value drivers differentiate one business from another and are critical tools for strategy. You have probably read about value drivers. They might show up in *Harvard Business Review* articles or in reports by consulting firms such as Deloitte and McKinsey. They are too rarely used in valuations and are the very heart of the QuickValue method. Though value drivers are subjective, they provide critical data that influence the value of a company and distinguish it from others. In many ways, a good assessment of a company's value drivers will give a complete picture of why a company is valued the way it is.

Rule 6. There's no such thing as an "average" company. Hence, valuations based on determining a single median are inherently flawed. When appraisers use market multiples, they generally find the median from a subset of multiples and declare that it should be used to value the company being analyzed. The problem with this approach is that if multiples for 15 companies are included in a valuation set, the company with the eighth highest multiple (the median) becomes the benchmark simply because it is in the middle. Think of how absurd it would be to line up by height 15 players on a basketball team to determine the height of players you should recruit. If the players range from six to seven feet tall, player 8 might be six feet, six inches. Using that median height as your sole guide, you would wind up with 15 players measuring six feet, six inches. Most likely, you'd also wind up with a losing record. What you really need, in sports or business, is the ability to alter your "lineup" based on understanding your specific strengths and weaknesses and knowing your greater goals.

QuickValue is designed specifically to meet these demanding criteria. Using this process, you will be able to:

- Conduct yearly valuations without disrupting your business operations.

- Do so using your own staff rather than outside appraisers.

- Confine your calculations to a single, straightforward method.

- Avoid making faulty financial projections.

- Better understand your most important value drivers, including both the positives and the areas that need work.

- And, finally, take confidence in knowing that in the end you'll have a valuation reflecting your unique business rather than some hypothetical average.

In Chapter 3, you'll get started by selecting just the right members for your QuickValue team. We'll discuss how to prep the team by communicating why the valuation process won't just make the company better—how it will help the members of the team improve their own individual performance. And we'll run through the targeted financial information you'll need to pull together to make it all happen.

Preparing Your Company for QuickValue

The idea behind QuickValue is that any midsize company can complete a valuation using internal staff, without disrupting regular operations. If you and your team commit to the process described in this book, you will come away with vital information that can help you grow strategically, stay on the right course, avoid unfortunate decisions, and understand your business at a level you may not have thought possible before. As with your favorite recipes, the final product is only going to be as good as the ingredients you put in.

We will walk through the essentials of building your QuickValue team and motivating its members to give the process their best effort. We'll talk about your role as owner or CEO and what you need to do (and *not* do) in order to make the process successful. Finally, we'll look at the internal data your team should pull together. Because QuickValue involves a single valuation method, the numbers you need aren't nearly as extensive as those needed for the external valuations we discussed in the previous chapter. Still, solid, reliable data are essential to getting an accurate result. Pulling these numbers together carefully will pay off in the end.

These preparations will take a little time and effort, especially when you use QuickValue for the first time. But keep in mind that this should become an annual process. By the second or third year, it will feel like a natural part of your operations, and the time investment should decrease accordingly.

Assembling Your QuickValue Team

QuickValue works best when a small handful of executives are involved in evaluating the business. Three or four of your best people is probably ideal. Any less, and the process could become myopic and most likely will not give you the range of creative and analytical skills and insights you need. Any more, and the process could become unwieldy. This is a team, not a committee.

If you have a chief strategy officer (CSO), that person may be the obvious choice to lead the team, since the CSO has a comprehensive view of the business and is directly responsible for working with the owner or CEO on implementing strategic goals. In my experience, though, most midsize businesses are a notch too small to have a designated CSO. If that is your situation, the best candidate is your most senior finance executive, whether chief financial officer, vice president of finance, or controller. Most likely, this individual already oversees your financial statements, annual budget, and strategic plan, all of which make the person a strong candidate to lead this effort as well. Then, fill out your team with a mix of creative and financial skills:

- **Creative input.** Ask yourself who the most dynamic and creative thinkers on your staff are. That could mean your head of sales or your product leader. These operating executives work on the front lines of a business. Your sales head, for example, will have a good idea how strong your product offerings are based on feedback from customers. Team members in financial roles may have greater difficulty assessing these characteristics. This is especially important during Step 1 (described in Chapter 4), in which you find and rate your company's most important value drivers. As you will see in Chapter 4, determining your value drivers requires a delicate combination of subjective vision and hard-nosed self-appraisal.

- **Analytics.** Your numbers people will come to the fore in Steps 2 and 3 (described in Chapters 5 and 6). That is when you determine the proper multiples to use and make precise calculations that yield your final result. For this role, your financial executive who leads the team may suffice, or you may support his or her skills with someone from manufacturing or distribution. Most of the work will fall on these executives. They will work with the financial statements and collect information about multiples from similar companies.

In the end, each company's team will look a little different. The objective is to wind up with three to four members with well-rounded, complementary skills and the ability to work together.

Pumping Them Up (and Managing Expectations)

The last thing your executives may want to hear is that you have another task for them. They are already swamped with day-to-day duties, not to mention long-term projects. Perhaps they've been involved in an external valuation at some point in their career and viewed it as a hassle with no upside for them. Anyone who has spent time in a business environment knows the difference between projects undertaken as one more bureaucratic headache versus those that inspire people. Those "headache" projects are seen as distractions. And people will mentally check out and grumble about getting back to their *real* work. To get the results you need, you must inspire your team, demonstrating why this process will be enlightening rather than burdensome. For example:

> **It will make the company stronger.** As senior executives, they have a vested interest in anything that gives the company a competitive edge and creates value. This is not about satisfying some external authority, nor is it purely about prepping the business for a sale and a big payday (this is where expectation management comes in). Explain that this is an internal undertaking to create a more prosperous company.

It will enhance their careers. They will have an inside look at how the company is managed and how it can be improved, all through the prism of value. QuickValue will change the way they make day-to-day decisions. They will evaluate each decision based on how it might impact long-term value. And they will become more effective managers in their current jobs and in any future positions they hold.

Membership is an honor. This is your A-team, your most trusted employees, with an important, outsized voice in shaping the destiny of the company.

It means a lot to you. Your top employees are experts at reading your signals. If you communicate your own passion and commitment, the members of your team will head home eager to share that they have been selected for a vital task.

Your Role as Owner or CEO

How actively you get involved in day-to-day deliberations will depend on a variety of factors, including the size and nature of your company, the expertise of your top staff, and how deeply you normally involve yourself in operations. Some owners will want to take part in all or most discussions. Others will leave the nuts and bolts to the team, asking only for updates followed by a detailed briefing when the process is complete. Either way, you should recognize and guard against the undue influence your presence can have, potentially skewing the results. This can happen in a number of ways.

QuickValue requires candid, even brutal, self-assessment. Since everyone in an organization has turf to protect, the team approach mitigates *self-assessment bias*—our tendency to give ourselves a break or to overvalue areas in which we are involved. For owners, your "area" is the whole company. That only magnifies the potential fallout from your biases. Some owners, for example, insist their companies are software as a service businesses (i.e., companies that host cloud-based software applications for customers to use) when in fact they belong in a different category entirely. Why do they believe this? Because SaaS companies are valued higher than most other businesses. These owners convince themselves that their companies have "SaaS-like" characteristics, whether they do or not. If you go into the QuickValue process with unrealistic ideas of what your business is or how well it performs, you will distort your valuation and undermine the process.

Keep in mind that while team members may feel comfortable pointing out faulty assumptions of their peers, they will be far less inclined to contradict a superior. I got my first taste of this back in college, when I interned in the planning department of a large corporation. I spent the summer helping create the department's first strategic plan, which included interviewing employees about our needs and researching how we matched up against competitors. By the end of the summer, the plan was finished. What I saw next shocked me. When the planning director presented our report to his superiors, he was told to adjust the results to match the head of the department's prior expectations. Never mind that the report we had worked on all summer—at considerable cost to the company—was based on careful research, whereas the department head's assumptions were based mainly on wishful thinking. Of course, this defeated the entire purpose of the project and deflated everyone who worked on it.

None of this means that you can't join the QuickValue team. Your knowledge and experience could make you a valuable member. But I strongly suggest that you not serve as leader. Leave that to your CSO or senior finance executive. And keep in mind that the more involved you are, the more incumbent it is upon you to recognize your potential biases (we all have them!) and assure other members that the goal is to reach an accurate valuation, not please the boss. So, let the chips fall where they may. Above all, avoid speculating about what you think the end value will be. If you let slip that you overheard from a friend that companies like yours sell for 12x EBITDA, your team will consciously or subconsciously view 12x EBITDA as its North Star.

Tapping Outside Expertise

In addition to your internal team, line up a trusted advisor or two to review your completed report as the last step before you finalize it. Ideally, these pros already know your business and may have a different perspective from that of the internal team—one that is worth hearing. By the time your team is finished, you will be so deep in the weeds that fresh eyes could expose oversights or inconsistencies. But note that these outside experts are not *part* of your QuickValue team. Involve them too early, and they may try to steer you to the traditional valuation methods they are most familiar with. They do not sit in on your meetings, and you are not bound to accept their advice. Still, they can be a valuable sounding board, point out things you may have overlooked, and help you keep the process honest and true.

Here are some possible candidates:

Accountants. If they prepare your financial statements and tax returns, accountants already understand your company, particularly its finances. Because they probably have many other clients, they may have a view of your company's relative performance.

Management consultants. If they have worked with you on projects, they know your business strategy. Perhaps they know whom you compete with, what your growth options are, and how your business performs compared with other companies in your market.

Investment bankers. Even if you do not have an investment banker on retainer, you may have one who has previously advised you, who has shown you M&A opportunities, or who knows your industry particularly well. These bankers may understand valuations in your industry from recent M&A transactions and will know why companies achieve the multiples they get.

The Financial Figures You'll Need

As you select and prep your QuickValue team, your finance team should be pulling together a short list of key financial information gathered from income statements and the balance sheet, along with owner perks and other extraordinary revenue and expenses.

Income statements. For best results, statements should be monthly (quarterly is OK, but monthly is preferred) and up to date. If you are going to prepare QuickValue in mid-September, measure your financial results through August 31. To get a full year of activity, you should measure from September 1 of the prior year to August 31 of the current year. If you keep financial results on a quarterly basis, make your cutoff the end of the most recent quarter. In this case it would be June 30, and your measurement period would be from July 1 of the prior year to June 30 of the current year.

Balance sheet. The balance sheet does not play a large role in QuickValue, but it will affect your value in a sale in many important ways. When a company is sold, balance sheet items such as excess cash, non-operating assets (company plane, securities, the cash-surrender value of a life insurance policy) or liabilities, and loans are either left with the seller or assumed by the buyer. Both scenarios affect sale proceeds. If you keep the cash and loans, the cash adds to your proceeds while the loans subtract from them. If the buyer assumes excess cash or loans, the purchase price is adjusted accordingly. For example, if the purchase price is $25 million and you have excess cash of $1 million and loans of $5 million, you will receive sale proceeds of $21 million ($25 million plus $1 million in cash minus $5 million in loans).

If your company has deferred revenue (payment for services or products you have not yet provided), buyers typically look for a price adjustment. That is because they will be stuck with the cost of providing services or products for which they will not receive income. If you own a building or other real estate, a real estate appraiser should value these separately. Often, buyers will not acquire any accompanying real estate because they may relocate the business to their own offices.

Finally, be aware that most M&A transactions have an adjustment for working capital. Working capital is calculated by subtracting current liabilities from current assets. Buyers want to buy an ongoing business that will not require a cash infusion the day after they buy it. They contend that the business should fund itself and that sellers should leave adequate working capital in the company to do so. If your business is deemed to have excess working capital, you keep it. If there is a working capital deficit, you'll need to fund it, or it will reduce your sale proceeds.

Florian von Alten, a managing partner at Oaklins in Hamburg, Germany, recalls how a balance sheet asset factored into a purchase price for a client. He was selling a security company serving airports and warehouses. The company was valuable because of its unique asset: thousands of German shepherd dogs trained to detect drugs, explosives, or other contraband in luggage or shipments. Yet because the dogs were expensive and the company acquired clients through public auctions, its EBITDA margins were squeezed. The company's auditors agreed to put the dogs on the balance sheet as an asset that would depreciate over time. By counting the dogs as a unique asset outside of the EBITDA multiple, Florian was able to convince the buyer to pay a higher price for the company than what could have been achieved using just an EBITDA multiple.

The reason balance sheet adjustments do not figure directly into the QuickValue calculations is that they are typically negotiated between a buyer and seller, as with the case above. Still, maintaining a clear, up-to-date balance sheet is a best practice for your business and will be essential when negotiating with a potential buyer. While you are taking care of the other items on this list, be sure to regularly monitor balance sheet items that could add to or subtract from your value and consider them when you need to calculate the net proceeds you may receive in a sale.

Owner perks and other extraordinary revenue and expenses. You should be aware of all personal items expensed to the company (often to reduce tax exposure) as well as any revenue or expenses that are extraordinary (non-operating or non-recurring)—in other words, not essential to your company's regular functions. As we'll discuss below, a careful accounting of these expenses is essential to an accurate EBITDA assessment.

Adhering to High Standards

That's it! You do not need most of the other information that outside appraisers require. No historical financial results. No pie-in-the-sky projections of future earnings. And no formal reports on operating metrics—after all, as employees, the members of your team already have this information at hand.

Yet while the number of documents you need is thankfully small, it pays to take special care in preparing them. So, let's go over some steps to help ensure you get the best results.

Use accrual accounting. The Internal Revenue Service permits private companies with revenue under $25 million to use cash accounting in their bookkeeping. Cash accounting records revenue and expenses at the time cash actually changes hands. Cash accounting is relatively simple and offers a straightforward way to monitor cash flow. That is why many smaller businesses use it, especially in the early going. Accrual accounting recognizes revenue and cost of goods when products or services are delivered to the customer, whether or not cash has been received. The accrual method, while more complex, more accurately reflects your revenue and expenses over time, offering a much clearer picture of your financial health.

QuickValue can only work if you use accrual accounting. In Chapter 5, when we compare multiples of public and private companies similar to yours, all those figures will come from businesses that use accrual accounting. Cash accounting can significantly inflate or reduce EBITDA. Thus, if you compare your own cash-based statements with other companies' accrual-based figures, your valuation will appear higher or lower than it should.

If you are using the cash method, have your accountants convert your financial statements to accrual before you undergo QuickValue. That transition could take three to five weeks. It's an investment that will pay off in the long run by positioning you to compete in the big leagues. In fact, accrual accounting is one of the core tenets of generally accepted accounting principles (GAAP). And when the time comes to sell your business, a prospective buyer will accept only accrual accounting when assessing its value.

Mind the GAAPs. Accounting, as with baseball, has its own rule book. In the mid- to late 1800s, the baseball gods determined that bases were to be 90 feet apart, that games would last nine innings, and that both teams would be allowed three outs for each inning. These and other standards have enabled baseball to maintain its fundamental integrity even as it developed into the global sport it is today. In the same way, accounting's GAAP rule book sets standards that can help a business grow with stability and integrity. The University of Alabama's business school offers a concise definition of five key GAAP principles:

1. **The revenue principle.** Revenue is earned and recorded at the point of sale, when the buyer takes possession of the item or service, not when the seller accepts the cash for the transaction.

2. **The expense principle.** An expense occurs when the business accepts goods or services from another entity, regardless of when it is billed or paid.

3. **The matching principle.** Each item of revenue should be matched with an item of expense. When you

apply the revenue, expense, and matching principles together, you are operating under the accrual accounting method.

4. **The cost principle.** Record the historical cost of an item in your financial statements, not the current value.

5. **The objectivity principle.** Use only factual, verifiable data in constructing your financial statements, never a subjective measurement of values.

The best way to determine if your financial statements are prepared in accordance with GAAP is to ask your accounting firm. If your statements are not prepared properly, the accounting firm can help fix them.

Another key financial step is to make sure you are correctly measuring EBITDA. EBITDA is the metric used to value the vast majority of businesses.[1] It became the standard metric for measuring the profitability of US companies in the mid- to late 1980s. The idea is to remove non-operating items, such as interest, taxes, depreciation, and amortization.

If you're like many midsize businesses, you may have to make a few adjustments to your EBITDA in order to arrive at numbers that accurately reflect your value. That is because midsize companies are often managed for the benefit of owners who are looking to minimize tax liability. Thus, profits on their financial statements may be lower than they would be for valuation purposes.

Review your expenses. This brings us back to those owner perks and other extraordinary (non-operating or non-recurring) revenue and expenses mentioned above. Owners sometimes expense cars, boats, home improvements, and personal travel to their businesses. Some may have their spouses, children, and other relatives on the payroll even though they are not needed by the business. Other owners take excess compensation above what a CEO or chairperson might take. While these expenses may make sense in terms of reducing your tax exposure, they make the company appear less profitable, and hence less valuable, than it actually is. You'll need to take these owner perks into account for valuation purposes. You must also remove other extraordinary items, including one-time non-recurring and non-operating revenue and expenses, from your calculation of EBITDA.

Take a look at the full rundown in Table 3.1 for a hypothetical business owner with numerous expenses being charged to the company. The combined add-backs for owner perks and other extraordinary expenses come to $1 million. When added back to the GAAP EBITDA of $6.5 million, the adjusted EBITDA (also known as pro forma EBITDA) is now 15 percent higher, or $7.5 million.

Of course, once you get started with add-backs, it is easy to go overboard. Every dollar you add back increases your value by whatever multiple your business is valued at (e.g., if your company is valued at 12x EBITDA, a $1,000 add-back increases your value by

TABLE 3.1 Sample Adjustments to EBITDA

EBITDA	$6,500,000
Owner Perks	
Car	50,000
Family members on payroll	250,000
Excess owner compensation	250,000
Owner's life insurance policy	50,000
Total Owner Perks	**$600,000**
Other Extraordinary Expenses	
Board fees	150,000
Lawsuit settlement (1-time)	250,000
Total Non-Operating Expenses	**$400,000**
Adjusted EBITDA	**$7,500,000**

$12,000), so it is tempting to be aggressive. Do not be overzealous. I once had a client who gave his staff a pizza party every Friday. When we were selling his company, he insisted that this expense should be an add-back. His reasoning was that the new owner would not need to spend money on pizza parties. The staff could do without them. The buyer came to a different conclusion. Because the pizza party had become a regular event, it was not an add-back. Even under new ownership the employees would expect to still have their pizza party. Err on the side of being conservative, and if an add-back seems questionable, it is probably best not to include it.

When to Prepare QuickValue

You can use QuickValue at any time of the year. For maximum impact, I recommend scheduling the process at a time when it can directly inform your annual budget and strategic planning. Your findings will provide observations that should be incorporated into both.

If your annual budget is prepared between October and December, the best window for creating QuickValue is between May and September. By mid-September, you should have quarterly financial results through June 30 and monthly financial results through August 31. If you decide to do your analysis earlier in the year, February or March is a good time. By then, you will have financial results for your previous calendar year through December 31.

With the team in place and on board with your mission and your financial timing determined, you're ready to use QuickValue. So, roll up your sleeves. In Chapter 4 we are going to dive into value drivers—the qualities that make your company unique, as well as the areas where you need to get better. First, let's take a look at how Sylvia A. organized her team to prepare a valuation.

Getting Metrics Mavens into QuickValue Shape

When we last checked in with Sylvia A., she had been given two weeks to respond to an exciting, unsolicited acquisition offer from a larger market research firm. Now, the race is on to determine whether the offer of 7.5x EBITDA is on target. Industry scuttlebutt suggests 7–10x EBITDA, so the offer *feels* about right. But with something this important, Sylvia wants to be sure.

Her first step is to gather a QuickValue team. Metrics Mavens is her baby, so she wants to be a part of the team effort. But she knows she is not the person to lead. The natural choice is the first person she turned to when the offer came in: CFO Joanna M. Joanna is smart, detail-oriented, and universally respected around the company. Joanna has a top-notch controller, Sarah S., who can be a big help with the information gathering and number crunching.

That is already a strong team, but something is missing. Sylvia wants someone who understands the broad sweep of the industry and can push the more numbers-oriented members of the team to think creatively. Her head of sales, Glenn B., comes to mind. Outgoing and gregarious, Glenn used to work in the consumer packaged goods industry and is deeply aware of what those companies (Metrics Mavens' core clients) want and need most. He knows everyone in the business, including the key competitors, and can offer essential insights on how Metrics Mavens stacks up. And he will not pull any punches.

Yet Sylvia also knows Glenn will be the toughest to pin down. He is notoriously independent, married to the road, and openly suspicious of "bean counters." Sure enough, when she raises the subject, he hems and haws and mutters something about "sales calls out the wazoo" through next quarter. "What do I know about valuation?" he protests. Sylvia explains what is at stake and insists she wants him on the team precisely because he is *not* a bean counter. He can be an invaluable part of identifying the company's value drivers. Whether or not Sylvia sells the company, Glenn's participation will make the company stronger and more valuable, she says. Instead of just selling products created by someone else, he can have a direct role in determining what those products should be. How could that help but make him a better head of sales? As Glenn listens, his protests soften. He is not doing cartwheels just yet, but he is ready to join the team.

Now is the time to get the financial statements in line. Fortunately, Joanna saw to it that the company implemented accrual accounting four years earlier amid a time of rapid growth. Joanna has also seen to it that the company is fully committed to GAAP. More reasons to love Joanna, Sylvia tells herself.

Now, about those owner perks and extraordinary revenue and expenses. In fairness to the valuation process, those items must be removed because they would not have occurred under a different owner. Since Metrics Mavens is owned entirely by Sylvia, she has typically had the company pay a small portion of her personal expenses. And there was also a one-time, non-recurring legal expense from a lawsuit. Removing these expenses would have the effect of increasing the company's EBITDA by the amount of the expenses. The prospective buyer offered a multiple of 7.5x EBITDA, so for each dollar of add-backs, Sylvia would be paid $7.50 in purchase price. Finding these expenses proves well worth the exercise.

A detailed analysis shows that the one-time legal expenses were $750,000 and the personal expenses for a new office in Sylvia's home were $250,000. Removing these expenses has the effect of adding $1 million to EBITDA. There are a couple of other items that feel like close calls. Revenue would have been higher by $100,000 if one client's new contract did not slip into the next year, for example. In the end, Joanna recommends not including those, just to be on the safe side. Nevertheless, she's able to share some good news with Sylvia: "We may have just added $7.5 million to the purchase price by increasing the adjusted EBITDA by $1 million." Just as important, the team now has solid, reliable financial numbers for the company—numbers the team can use to determine the company's actual value.

PART TWO

DISCOVER YOUR VALUE IN THREE STEPS

CHAPTER 4

Step 1. Find and Rate Your Value Drivers

Regardless of your industry or competitors, there is no business exactly like yours. While an outsider might see another midsize widget company, you and your team have a privileged understanding of what makes it different. It could be the formula developed by an ancestor 58 years ago and closely guarded ever since, or possibly it's the painstaking manufacturing process that other companies skimp on. Perhaps your business model is such that growth potential seems unlimited, and steady profit margins year to year have proved your ability to surmount the most difficult economic conditions. You also have challenges—trouble finding workers in your area to fill the skilled positions, a need to get your products to market faster, or an overreliance on one or two customers.

Your intimate knowledge of these pros and cons is your greatest asset in determining your company's worth. When you sit down and evaluate them in a systematic way, these seemingly amorphous qualities can be transformed into *value drivers*—hard evidence supporting the value of your business.

Value drivers are not a new concept, of course. Sophisticated buyers will be analyzing your value drivers as they decide whether to buy your business and for how much. As chief digital officer for the German digital media company Axel Springer, Jens Mueffelmann oversaw more than 100 acquisitions. Value drivers, the qualitative part of his analysis, were hugely influential in determining whether to do a deal. The quantitative part, valuation models, was simply a way to support his decisions, he recalls. Ken Collins, one of my former Oaklins partners, echoes this sentiment: "Value drivers are those soft, intangible elements that are often overlooked but are critical to driving value beyond mathematical formulas."

Investment bankers have used value drivers for years to help companies assess their strengths and get better. Peter Gray, a partner at our Oaklins office in London, provides prospective clients with a list of value drivers (reproduced in Table 4.1) to consider before putting their business up for sale. It's a strong list. Any company of any kind would do well to improve in the areas Peter describes.

QuickValue elevates and enhances the concept of value drivers in three key ways. First, you will develop a list of value drivers customized not just to your industry but to your specific company. Second, QuickValue incorporates value drivers

TABLE 4.1   Peter Gray's Checklist of Value Drivers for a Sale

Market Position Defendable, differentiated position in an attractive market Market leader in niche High barriers to entry Strong, unique intellectual property Best strategic fit with buyer

Strategy
Robust growth strategy based on track record
Scalable platform that can be:
  • Further developed at minimal cost
  • Rolled out geographically

People Management team for private equity or succession Depth of management
Operations/Technology Best in class key performance indicators for sector Digitally transformed Excellent technology platform
Financials Attractive revenue and EBITDA growth Strong recurring revenues; contracted revenue stream Clean corporate structure Detailed, up-to-date, timely financial information
Customer Diversified and loyal client base Highly rated by customers Strong brand recognition

Source: Oaklins Cavendish.

directly into your calculations. You'll score each one independently and use the results to help determine your company's specific value. And third, you will create a powerful resource to help feed your company's growth strategy.

Through decades of buying, selling, and working closely with owners of midsize businesses, I have developed a list of 45 value drivers: 45 essential qualities that emerge again and again.

In this chapter, we will walk through all the value drivers. We will look at how you and your team can narrow the list to those most essential to your company. You will rate each one individually, and then calculate your Value Driver Score—the first step in determining your company's worth. If you believe your business is dependent on a value driver that is not on the list, feel free to include it in your assessment using the same formula discussed below. And please let me know what that new value driver you have uncovered is. I will consider adding it to the list at www.quickvaluemethod.com.

Find Your Value Drivers

As you consider the 45 possibilities listed below, how will you know *your* value drivers—the ones that best apply to your individual company? Think of the baseball scout who needs to evaluate a pitcher. He might have a checklist of questions: How hard does he throw? Does he have good control of the strike zone? Does he have the stamina to pitch for several innings? These are important characteristics to evaluate for just about any pitcher. Likewise, some of the value drivers on the list below—such as market share, profitability, and barriers to entry—will apply to just about any company, including, most likely, yours.

But then the baseball scout digs a little deeper, looking to evaluate individual characteristics that make this pitcher different from the others—the qualities that give a player a noticeable edge that could lead to a long Major League career—or that could pose difficulties on the road to success. Does his wicked sinker separate him from the pack? Does his arsenal include a knuckleball that ties power hitters up in knots? Are there any warning signs, such as a history of blowing up under pressure, or a series of nagging injuries that keep him out of action for weeks at a time?

Your task is to analyze an entire company rather than a single player. To help you identify those qualities most pertinent to your business, put yourself in the shoes of a potential investor or buyer. Many of the descriptions below are framed in just those terms—what investors are concerned about. You will be amazed at how your perception of your business changes at the thought of putting your hard-earned money into buying the business. You will become more critical and less forgiving in your assessment, which is exactly what is needed in choosing the right value drivers.

Your value drivers list is not a greatest hits album, nor a victory lap. While outstanding qualities have an important place here, so too (and perhaps especially) do your rough spots—areas that keep you up at night. Every company has them, and the more objective you can be in assessing them, the more valuable this process will be. Honesty about flaws will make you stronger for years to come.

So, get out a pen and mark this section up. Check the value drivers most pertinent to your company. I have grouped them into broad categories familiar to most businesspeople. Drivers marked with ★★ are "key value drivers" that you should give special attention to, since they're likely to apply to any company. At this point, do not worry if you wind up with 20 or 25 on your initial list. You can whittle down from there. I suggest that you include at least 5 of these key value drivers on your list because they are so critical. Some valuation experts are even more adamant about the importance of key value drivers. David Orth, of Citizens Capital Markets, believes that considerations such as revenue stability (value driver 5), profitability and return on invested capital (value driver 6), brand equity (value driver 11), and competition (value driver 14) warrant a place on any list. But the list, ultimately, is up to you. Later in the chapter, you will drill down to the 8 to 12 that are absolutely essential, rate each on a scale of 0 to 10, and calculate your company's Value Driver Score—a key component for determining your overall value.

The List

Your Market

Value driver 1: ★★ Market size and potential value. Consider the overall market for your products or services. Consumable products such as toilet paper represent a vast market, whereas the market for personal aircraft is small. That does not mean private planes are a bad business, but even under the best conditions, buyers represent a small percentage of the population, whereas everybody needs paper products. Another key consideration is the potential value you stand to create for your owners and shareholders. After closely analyzing Instagram, Facebook paid $1 billion for a company that at the time had yet to produce revenue. Why? Because users were growing so fast that Instagram had the potential to become as large as Facebook. As Dan McCarthy, CEO of Dodge Data & Analytics, notes, "Market size has a massive impact on how investors think about a company."

Value driver 2: Market trends. Is your market growing or declining? Are there changes coming that could impact your business? Within the media industry, filmed entertainment is ascending to meet high consumer demand for streaming services, while print media is in decline because of heated competition from digital options. Similar trends in your market will directly affect your valuation.

Business Model

Value driver 3: Business premise. Do you have a good business thesis and a plan for the future, or are you hanging on in a legacy business whose best days are behind it? Are you a challenger or an incumbent, and what does each mean for your growth plan? To value your business highly, investors must be convinced that your business is sustainable. A clear, honest appraisal of your business premise could help you make key decisions about the company's value—and your direction for the future.

Value driver 4: ★★ Intellectual property. Do you have patents, trademarks or unique business processes, or content protected by copyrights? These protections help create a moat around your business that makes it hard for competitors to breach. As such, these protections add to the overall value of your business. In the world of investments, intellectual property is considered important enough that there are full-time appraisers who specialize in valuing these assets.

Value driver 5: ★★ Revenue stability. Does your revenue remain consistent or vary widely from year to year? Stable revenue implies consistent sales. Note that "stable" and "consistent" do not mean "flat." Steady growth is fantastic. Predictability is what investors want. It adds to your value by removing risk. What concerns investors (and could affect the value of your enterprise) is revenue that fluctuates wildly. A classic example is film production, where this year's blockbuster may be followed by next year's flop. Valērija Lieģe, a partner with the Oaklins team in the Baltics, recently advised a fast-growing construction company. Its EBITDA quadrupled in two years and was expected to double in the next two years. Despite this impressive growth, contracts with clients were large, and the procurement process created revenue uncertainties. Because of this, buyers anticipated unstable revenue growth, and the business, despite its rapid growth, sold at a discount.

Value driver 6: ★★ Profitability and return on invested capital. How profitable is your business, and is it organized in a way that you can achieve good returns on your investments? Are you good at controlling overhead costs? How efficient are you at making money? Highly profitable businesses are less risky, and investors reward lower risk with higher valuations. Those with 30 percent EBITDA margins are almost always more valuable than businesses with 5 percent EBITDA margins. A reduction in sales might barely impact the profitability of the company with a 30 percent EBITDA margin, whereas the same decline could be debilitating to a lower-margin business.

Value driver 7: Core competencies. What capabilities does your company have that make your business work? Do you have a creative team with skills that are superior to your competitors' skills? Maybe you have the best software engineers in your industry. A clear list of core competencies (or the lack thereof) says a lot about your viability within your industry.

Value driver 8: ★★ Barriers to entry. If somebody else wanted to jump into your business tomorrow, what obstacles would the person face? Is your product especially difficult to make, or are there regulations or required approvals that limit competition? A classic example is utilities. Charles Firlotte, a former water company CEO, notes that while utilities may have limited growth potential, close regulation and the need for substantial capital investments on a regular basis create effective barriers to entry. As a caveat, Firlotte notes that traditional barriers may not always tell the whole story (see value driver 14, below). Other businesses enjoy protection through exclusivity contracts. Valērija Lieģe advised a company that held exclusive rights to distribute a premium car brand. When the company was sold, the buyer was willing to pay a premium because he already knew how valuable the distribution rights were in blocking competition. At the other end of the spectrum, restaurants and other service industries often have far fewer barriers to entry and face fierce competition.

Value driver 9: Economies of scale. Do you have special advantages in your operation that allow you to grow your business more efficiently than your competitors? Typically, these occur in manufacturing businesses. If a unit costs $1.50 to produce and your production doubles, will your cost per unit decline to $1.00? As your output increases, the ability to lower your cost per unit will be highly regarded by investors and thus add to your value.

Value driver 10: Visibility of future revenue. Do you have a sales pipeline that stretches into the future? How far can you predict your revenue? Recurring revenue is highly prized by investors because it locks in earnings and removes the risk that your business could decline overnight. It also makes your business less dependent on finding new customers.

Company Profile

Value driver 11: ★★ Brand equity. How well is your brand known by customers and prospects? As with intellectual property (value driver 4), brand equity discourages competition. The concept is somewhat amorphous because, unlike with revenue, there is no specific number that corresponds to brand equity. Yet it is real and potentially powerful because of the loyalty and affinity it manifests in customers. Perhaps you are old enough to remember the adage "Nobody ever got fired for buying IBM." Likewise, Kleenex and Coca-Cola are such powerful brands that their names are often used generically in place of facial tissues or colas. When Jens Mueffelmann, now executive chairman of Bonnier Corporation and formerly of Axel Springer, oversaw the sale of several high-profile US magazines, he said he and his colleagues underestimated the value of the brands, even in the struggling magazine industry. Buyers saw great potential for *Popular Science*, *Field & Stream*, *Outdoor Life*, and *Saveur* and were willing to pay up for them. At the same time, history shows that unforeseen crises, especially when mishandled, can diminish even sturdy brands. Consideration of brand equity should include the plans you have in place for risk and crisis management.

Value driver 12: Culture. Can you define what your culture is and why employees find it attractive? Is your company a champion of diversity? Does it support causes that are important to your employees? Millennials, especially, emphasize culture and want to work at companies with which they are proud to associate. And research increasingly suggests that companies viewed as good corporate citizens may do better financially than those that are not.

Value driver 13: Organization infrastructure. Are you organized in a way that allows you to respond to challenges with agility and resilience? Does your existing staff have enough bandwidth to take on new projects? Or would you need to expand your capabilities as you grow? While all companies change in some ways as they grow, investors look favorably upon those with a built-in "platform" available for expansion, especially if costs remain constant.

Value driver 14: ★★ Competition. This one belongs at the forefront of value drivers and is one of the first things investors want to know about a business. Do you have competitors, and if so, how many? Where do you rank among the competition, and do you have competitive advantages that give you an edge? Are you the market leader or in the middle or bottom of your industry? This is one of those areas where you must be especially careful to put pride and sentiment aside and think objectively. Also, consider the intensity of your competition. Are you in a dogfight, or do you have the market to yourself? Are there any nontraditional competitors that might move in on your business? Charles Firlotte, the former water company CEO, says not even utilities can afford complacency in a rapidly changing economy. Though barriers to entry (value driver 8) offer protection from traditional competitors, "the emerging competition for energy and electric utilities will be from nontraditional sources ranging from digital players such as Apple to Mrs. Smith down the street as she absorbs energy from her solar panels."

Value driver 15: Innovation. In value driver 4, we addressed your existing intellectual property. The ability to continually refine your products and services and develop new ones represents another big plus. Innovation is more important now than ever, when the life cycle of products and services is shorter. Companies that innovate and spend appropriately on research and development can prevent extinction.

Value driver 16: ★★ Growth dynamics and scalability. A key requirement for a good investment is growth. Its twin is scalability. Can you add new products or services, expand your geographic footprint to other countries, and/or grow your existing business without being overwhelmed? Over the years I have seen way too many companies with great ideas and innovative products fail because they were not adequately prepared when success called their name. That is why those two qualities—growth and scalability— are what investors look for when placing bets on companies. Benny Chung, a partner at our Oaklins firm in Hong Kong, worked with a client looking to expand its retail footprint to the world's largest market, China. Chung's client already owned retail outlets in the United Kingdom and entered China through a minority investment in a large department store operator in China.

Products and Services

Value driver 17: ★★ Market share. As a rule, the more of your market you control, the greater your valuation will be. Market share is one of the key value drivers and almost certainly deserves a place on your list. Our first value driver, market size and potential value, assessed your future prospects, based on the size and potential growth of your overall market. This value driver, market share, evaluates what portion of the market you have already captured, as measured by revenue or units. Investors like to acquire companies with dominant market share because it gives them a solid foundation from which to expand into other businesses or industries.

Value driver 18: Product life cycle. Consider how many years your flagship products have remaining in their life cycle. At what point will they need to be replaced or risk becoming defunct? A longer life span removes risk from your business and increases your value.

Value driver 19: Pricing power. The ability to raise prices without a significant decline in sales indicates pricing power. Investors prefer companies that can increase prices rather than those whose sales are highly sensitive to pricing.

Value driver 20: Supply chain. Do you have reliable access to the essential materials you need to manufacture your products and operate your business? What are your contingency plans in case your usual supply chains are disrupted? As the coronavirus pandemic made clear, companies that are overly reliant on a single supplier or country are vulnerable.

Value driver 21: Manufacturing quality. Are your products of high quality? Try to take emotion and pride out of the equation when you consider this question. Frequent customer complaints about quality will diminish your value and make your business more vulnerable to competition.

Value driver 22: Store locations and distribution channels. How do you get your products or services to market? Do you have many options or just a few? Do you have great physical locations for your stores, or are they in low-traffic areas? Better locations and broader distribution channels add to your value.

Value driver 23: Time to market. How quickly can you get finished products or services to market? What is the average for your industry, and how do you compare? This will be more vital for some industries than others. If you are involved with smartphones, for example, your customers can't wait to get their hands on the most updated features. Do you have the capability to shorten your timeline, thus giving you a competitive advantage?

Your Team

Value driver 24: ★★ Leadership. This quality is among the most delicate for you and your team and among the most important to assess as objectively as possible. Smart, successful, and admired leaders are worth their weight in gold. At Oaklins in 2020, we sold a New York–based social impact agency called Purpose. Though the company was not well known, its CEO, Jeremy Heimans, had recently coauthored a bestselling book, *New Power: How Power Works in Our Hyperconnected World—and How to Make It Work for You*. CEOs and philanthropists alike sought coauthor Heimans's insights. His star power and leadership skills added to the value of the company and were key factors in Purpose commanding an outsized price when the sale went through. By contrast, a leader with good technical skills but no ability to inspire others can be a liability. Also, do you have a clear succession plan? Leadership is likely a key part of your valuation and is often considered in combination with the next value driver, management team.

Value driver 25: Management team. Are you overly dependent on one senior executive, or does a deep bench support her? If you lose some team members, can others take their place without missing a beat? How committed are the members of the management team? Do they have long-term contracts tied to the performance of your business, or are they simply working for a wage? Investors look for teams motivated to stay and build a strong business. By now, you are probably familiar with the term "acquihire" (or "acqui-hire"). That is when a company is sold because of the value of its management team and highly skilled employees. Engineers have been particularly attractive to technology companies in recent years. Florian von Alten, of Oaklins in Germany, sold an industrial automation company that had 400 engineers who were highly compensated. Their wages made the company's EBITDA margins less impressive. So Florian convinced buyers how expensive and time-consuming it would be to have to hire headhunters to replicate the management and engineering teams. This strategy led to an increased purchase price on top of what the company was worth based solely on its EBITDA.

Value driver 26: Labor pool. Do you have access to the right population for future employees? Do they have the skills you need? What is the competition like for the best employees? Companies located in close proximity to college towns such as Ann Arbor, Michigan; Austin, Texas; and Boulder, Colorado, may have an edge in attracting a regular supply of recent graduates, compared with a company with operations far removed from the nearest great campus.

Value driver 27: Employee satisfaction. Just as important as attracting employees is holding onto them. Are yours enthusiastic and committed to your success? What is your turnover rate? What is your rating on Glassdoor? In an age when any prospect can research your company with a few simple searches, satisfaction of existing employees is a key factor in attracting new ones. Companies on "100 Best Places to Work" lists have an advantage in hiring the employees they want.

Customer Relationships

Value driver 28: Quality of the customer base. If you cater mainly to other businesses, are they blue chip or outfits nobody has heard of? Marquee brands help demonstrate stability and growth potential and give comfort to prospective customers who are evaluating you. If your customers are consumers, are their demographics attractive? Do they have money to spend, or is price sensitivity the driving concern? The quality of your customer base could influence your valuation.

Value driver 29: Customer engagement. What is the average tenure for your clients or customers? Is your renewal rate high, or do customers consistently drop away and need to be replenished? Engaged and committed customers are valuable to any business.

Value driver 30: Customer diversity. Are you dependent on a few clients who represent most of your revenue? This could expose your business to sudden decreases in revenue and profits. I recall one impressive company that my firm was involved in selling. Its one drawback: 80 percent of revenue came from a single customer. Though that customer was blue chip, the risk of losing 80 percent of revenue at once caused many potential suitors to drop out. Ultimately, we did find an attractive buyer, but the delay and reduced valuation attested to the importance of customer diversity.

Value driver 31: Customer experience. How do customers rate your business, and what level of trust do your relationships generate? Is that rating improving or declining? Is your customer experience seamless across online and offline interactions? How robust is your customer service? Companies have realized how important delivering a good experience is to their customers, and investors hold companies to the same high standard.

Value driver 32: Customer acquisition cost. Does it take weeks or months of wooing to land new clients or customers, or do *they* actively seek out your products and expertise? While every business model differs, the less time and money you spend on customer acquisition, the higher your profit margins and the more attractive you are likely to be to investors.

Third-Party Relationships

Value driver 33: Joint venture partners and strategic alliances. Do you have partners who make your business more effective? There is the magic formula where one plus one equals *three*, when each party brings something important to the relationship and helps create a stronger whole. Solid partnerships with a record of success add value to your company. But be wary of becoming overly dependent upon any single partnership, as a disruption in that relationship could significantly affect your business. Buyers will assess both the benefit of and the reliance on partnerships when determining the value of your company.

Value driver 34: Vendor relationships. Are your contracts with vendors favorable or onerous? Do you have good relationships with your vendors? In a crisis, will you get priority over others? Favorable vendor relationships can include attractive pricing, flexibility on payment terms, or having the vendor's A-team rather than B-team assigned to your company.

Value driver 35: Licensing partners. Many businesses make significant profits by licensing their intellectual property to others. The Walt Disney Company, for example, is the largest licensor in the world, selling more than $55 billion in products through its licensees. These relationships greatly enhance the value of Disney.[1] Even smaller companies can make licensing work: BuzzFeed launched its licensing business in 2017 and generated less than $5 million in sales, but that increased to $260 million by 2019.[2]

Value driver 36: Franchisor-franchisee relationships. This value driver will apply only to certain businesses, but if your model depends on your relationship with a franchisor, it is likely an important part of your list. Does your relationship tell a story of cordial relations, steady growth, and mutual benefit, or has it been strained by conflicts? Is the franchisor a well-regarded company in its own right, or has it struggled? These questions will have an important influence on your value.

Value driver 37: Advisors. Is the guru in the industry part of your team? Board members and consultants can add value to your business. The book *Trillion Dollar Coach: The Leadership Playbook of Silicon Valley's Bill Campbell* makes abundantly clear how much influence an advisor can have on a company. Campbell was considered to be invaluable to the success of both Google and Apple.

Finance and Planning

Value driver 38: Reliable financial planning and reporting. Too many midsize companies get so caught up in creating and selling great products that they treat their finances as an afterthought. Yet investors know that sound financial management is essential to any company's success, and they view poor financial systems as a significant risk that decreases value. By contrast, companies with a strategic plan, audited financials, and an annual budget gain credibility with investors.

Value driver 39: Acquisition expertise. Is your team skilled at acquiring businesses? Does your team have experience doing so? Investors covet smart teams that can perform efficient tuck-in acquisitions. Many companies owned by private equity investors create value by acquiring other businesses and making them more valuable through integration.

Value driver 40: Financial controls. How good are your financial controls? When we performed due diligence for the sale of a client's company, it became clear that the CEO was embezzling funds. Not surprisingly, that put a serious damper on the deal as prospective buyers wondered if there were other financial irregularities.

Value driver 41: Capital requirements. Does your business have high or low capital expenditure requirements? Businesses with low capital requirements for day-to-day operations are more attractive to investors because they free up capital for other purposes.

Value driver 42: Access to capital. Midsize companies may have limited options in tapping additional capital, whether in the form of equity or debt. Do the principals in your company have deep pockets and a willingness to invest more? Do you have an established credit line with your bank? If you have solved for this, you are better positioned to take advantage of growth opportunities, including investments and acquisitions. You will also be less likely to be compelled to compromise your standards out of necessity or desperation.

Investments

Value driver 43: Technology and R&D. Is your technology up to date or in need of an overhaul? Have you invested enough in R&D to protect future revenue? If you are a drug company, research and development are a precursor to your future product line, and this value driver is critical to your success. Investors like to see companies that have consistently invested in R&D.

Value driver 44: Growth investments. Do you have investments in new businesses that could bring future value to your company? Alphabet has made many bets on new businesses that are different from Google and that could add tremendous value to the parent company. Unlike acquisitions, these new business possibilities are incubated within your company.

Value driver 45: Cybersecurity. Another key consideration is the effectiveness of your systems for handling cybersecurity risks. In an age when hackers may strike from within your own walls or from the other side of the world, the safety of your business, your clients, and your reputation relies on investing in robust defenses.

Hone Your List

Here is where you get to the nitty-gritty—paring your value drivers down to the 8 to 12 that are most vital to your operations. These will vary for every business. Consider value driver 18: product life cycle. If you are a technology company, a product life span of five years compared with an industry average of two years could be a critical competitive advantage—and a boost to your value. Or if you have to reinvent your line every year, that could spell trouble. Either way, life cycle is likely important to include on your list. But what if, instead, you make artisan Parmigiana-Reggiano cheese? Value drivers such as core competencies (value driver 7), supply chain (value driver 20), or manufacturing quality (value driver 21) may be key considerations, but life cycle is hardly a factor for a product that dates back to the Middle Ages. Pick the value drivers that are most relevant, not just the ones where you will score the highest.

Of course, not all your decisions are going to be that straightforward. But healthy disagreement and spirited debate are part of the process—and part of the fun. Set aside several hours. Pull up chairs and engage your team. The close calls may be the most revealing parts of your discussion. You will be amazed by what you learn that can inform your everyday decision-making. Your final list can serve as the backbone for your growth strategy, for instance, by identifying holes in your capabilities or by highlighting a potential competitor that you are not currently paying attention to.

As you hone your list, keep your "investor hat" on and think of your business as a potential buyer would. That will help you zero in on the value drivers that, in fact, influence your value the most.

It bears repeating that value drivers are both positive and negative, meaning they add to your value or subtract from it. What works well and what does not? Things you do not do well will decrease your valuation. But remember—this is for your benefit. The challenges you acknowledge right now will only help you get stronger as a company.

A final list of 10 value drivers is a good target but not set in stone. Fewer than 8 is probably not enough because you might end up placing too much emphasis on too few qualities. More than 12 becomes unwieldy, and you risk watering down the impact of the most important ones on your list. Just make sure that every driver you choose is essential to your operations.

Rate Your Value Drivers

Once you have a firm list, you can begin to score yourself on each value driver. QuickValue uses a scale from 0 to 10, with 9 or

10 representing the areas where you are truly exceptional and 0 to 2 representing the areas where you need the most work.

While your goal for each driver is a simple number that you can use in calculating your Value Driver Score, do not take the ratings lightly or make snap decisions. Give ratings the same thought, analysis, and debate that your team put into creating your list. Do a SWOT analysis. You are probably familiar with the term "SWOT"—business school lingo for "strengths, weaknesses, opportunities, and threats." A SWOT analysis usually involves a review of your entire operation. Here you need to zero in on one value driver at a time, almost as though that quality were its own individual company.

Consider, for example, market share (value driver 17). If you control just 3 percent of the market and many companies rank ahead of you, you have identified a real weakness. You might rate a 1 or 2. But perhaps you are in the process of rolling out an exciting new product, or maybe you are about to shake hands on an acquisition or you have recently heard that a venerable competitor is shutting down. Each of these presents an imminent market opportunity that should be reflected in a higher rating. By the same token, a 65 percent market share could put you at the top of the heap among your competitors, justifying a rating of 9 to 10. But if your share was 67 percent last year and 85 percent five years ago, a superlative rating might be an exercise in denial of threats that are already endangering your leadership. Generally, market share should be relatively easy to score because the total market size is quantifiable. If you do not have that information at hand, consider compiling a list of your competitors and ascribing revenue estimates for each as a way to help determine your relative size in the market.

Other value drivers, such as business premise (value driver 3), are more subjective and may take a bit more thinking. Still, your business premise can be an important indicator of where you are headed as a company. Say, for example, you are a midsize manufacturer of medical equipment. During the global coronavirus pandemic, as some industries struggled, orders for your personal protective equipment (PPE) soared to the point that you could barely keep up. Though PPE had been just one of several product lines, after March 2020, when the virus swept the country, it became the major priority. How did your business premise change? And what is your long-term outlook? Will a heightened focus on health and hygiene support that intensified focus on PPE, or will you need to reset your premise as the pandemic fades into the history books?

In Chapter 9, we will look at how SWOT analyses of your value drivers can help your strategic planning. For now, the main goal is to rate each driver as carefully and accurately as you can. Give each value driver on your final list an individual number, as follows, based on whether your company is exceptional, above average, average, below average, or unexceptional in that area. Though the ratings are up to you, keep in mind that absolute, even brutal, honesty will pay off in the end by revealing the areas you most need to improve.

Rating

9–10: Exceptional

7–8: Above average

5–6: Average

3–4: Below average

0–2: Unexceptional

Even on this select list, not all your value drivers are created equal. So, there is one more rating step, prioritizing the list by "important," "very important," and "critical." Critical drivers receive triple weighting, and very important ones receive double weighting. The rest of the individual scores count once. Note that the key value drivers on your list are likely good candidates for extra weighting.

Critical: 3x

Very important: 2x

Important: 1x

Say, for example, that you rate your company an 8 on growth investments (value driver 44). If that area is critical to your business, its triple weighting brings that score to 24 (out of a possible 30). If intellectual property is very important and you recognize your deficiency in this area with a low score of 3, that double weighting generates a score of 6 (out of 20). In both cases (positive and negative), the extra weighting will have an outsized impact on your value.

Once you have rated your value drivers on a scale of 0 to 10 and applied extra weighting to the ones that deserve it, you are ready to determine your Value Driver Score. Adding up your score and dividing by the maximum possible score will give you an overall score, expressed as a percentage:

81–100 percent: Exceptional

61–80 percent: Above average

41–60 percent: Average

21–40 percent: Below average

0–20 percent: Unexceptional

For example, if you started with 11 value drivers and deemed 2 to be critical, you have a maximum of 150 points (2 at 3x for 60 points, and 9 at 1x for 90 points). If your ratings add up to 45, then your Value Driver Score is 30 percent (45 divided by 150), which is below average. Hold onto that Value Driver Score. In Chapter 5, we will use it to help determine the next crucial consideration—your marketplace multiples.

Metrics Mavens Finds Its Value Drivers

With an offer for the company on the table and the clock ticking, Sylvia, Joanna, and the rest of the team set aside a full day to carefully evaluate all 45 value drivers. Some they are able to eliminate right away: Since the company is a research and data firm, the team is not concerned with supply chain (value driver 20) or manufacturing quality (value driver 21). Since the company is not a franchise, value driver 36 does not apply. And the company is too young for acquisition expertise (value driver 39) to be a factor.

Others, such as financial controls (value driver 40), reliable financial planning and reporting (value driver 38), and customer acquisition cost (value driver 32), are serious contenders. Each has its champions during the discussion and debate. But in the end, the following 10 value drivers, 5 of which are key value drivers, win out. Here's how it breaks down:

#1 Intellectual property (value driver 4). The patented technology Sylvia developed is widely recognized as Metrics Mavens' most valuable asset. It does not simply make the list; it is critical enough to warrant a triple weighting. **Scoring:** 8 points, times 3, for a total of 24 of a possible 30 points.

#2 Quality of the customer base (value driver 28). Metrics Mavens has blue chip customers in the consumer packaged goods industry that competitors covet, so this value driver's score receives double weighting. **Scoring:** 8 points, times 2, for a total 16 of 20 possible points.

#3 Growth dynamics and scalability (value driver 16). This score would be higher if the business had evolved to serving markets beyond consumer packaged goods. Growth has been good but not great, and this value driver is important enough that the team gives it a double weighting. **Scoring:** 7 points, times 2, for a total 14 points of 20 possible points.

#4 Competition (value driver 14). Despite Metrics Mavens' intellectual property advantage, two strong competitors have entered the space and are giving the company fits. Glenn, the sales manager, notes that four years ago virtually every customer told him Metrics Mavens was the only research firm they would consider. These days, more and more are raising the names of these competitors and asking why Metrics Mavens is worth the higher price. Glenn does not believe this constitutes an emergency—yet. But rising competition is something the team needs to stay on top of. So, this value driver makes the list, and the team gives itself only an average grade. **Scoring:** 5 points of 10 possible points.

#5 Revenue stability (value driver 5). Revenue has remained remarkably stable for the past three years, and there are contracts in place to ensure continued stability into next year, making this one of the company's best features. **Scoring:** 9 of 10 possible points.

#6 Leadership (value driver 24). Though she is an excellent researcher, Sylvia is the first to admit she is more comfortable managing numbers than people, and the team feels empowered to give her a middling rating. **Scoring:** 4 of 10 possible points.

#7 Market trends (value driver 2). The company's focus on social listening is in demand by clients, and growth prospects are good. This is one of the factors softening Glenn's fears about competition. **Scoring:** 8 of 10 possible points.

#8 Pricing power (value driver 19). Still, those pesky competitors are limiting the company's ability to increase prices. **Scoring:** 3 of 10 possible points.

#9 Customer experience (value driver 31). Though the company's product is second to none, the human touch (or lack thereof) has always been a problem area, with numerous complaints about customer service. When Sylvia says, "I think we're getting a lot better since we upgraded our automated response system," Glenn lets out an audible sigh. "No offense, but this is my biggest headache," he says. "We bust our hump to make a sale, and three months later we're on the phone with a customer griping that he can't get support. People want a human voice, not a robot." **Scoring:** 2 of 10 possible points.

#10 Advisors (value driver 37). Sylvia recruited top professors from her university who refer clients to her and help advise Metrics Mavens. Their involvement in the business has been invaluable. **Scoring:** 8 of 10 possible points.

The combined scores total 93 points of a possible 140. Dividing 93 by 140 produces a Value Driver Score of 66 percent. To be an exceptional company, Metrics Mavens would have to score between 81 and 100 percent. Still, 66 percent is above average, and Joanna and her team are pleased. Just going through such a detailed review gives them an immediate benefit of an even greater understanding of their company, with clear ideas about where to focus on improvements. And in a single day they have already completed the first major step in understanding the value of their company.

CHAPTER 5

Step 2. Determine Your Multiples Range

Take a moment to celebrate what you and your team have already accomplished. By diving methodically into your value drivers, you have gained new insight into your company. You understand at a deeper level what your customers value most and what they wish you would do better. If you stop right now, you have information that can help you grow strategically and concentrate your resources where they can do the most good. Congratulations—but don't stop yet!

The next step in determining your value is to find out how you stack up against similar businesses. We will accomplish this through a careful analysis of market multiples, including stocks of publicly held companies, as well as transactions involving private firms. Public companies are easier to assess because the US

Securities and Exchange Commission and similar regulatory agencies in other countries require them to disclose their financial information. For private transactions you will need to do some investigating. That may sound like difficult information to come by, but you can find it surprisingly easily if you know where to look.

Both types of comparable companies—public and private—have advantages and drawbacks when used in your valuation process. While it may seem counterintuitive, the starring role goes to public companies, with private transactions playing a significant but supporting role. In a moment, we will see why. Capturing the advantages of each while accounting for their shortcomings requires some precise calculations. Your finance team will contribute most heavily in this chapter. We will carefully walk through each calculation. By the end, you will have clear numbers that, when used in conjunction with your Value Driver Score from Chapter 4, will give you the valuation you are after.

Why Market Multiples?

You may be wondering why market multiples deserve such a prominent place in valuation, and why they are superior to the traditional valuation methods described in Chapter 3. Quite simply, they are more accurate and easier to use. As Shannon Pratt, one of the leading valuation experts of the twentieth century, wrote: "The market approach is a pragmatic way to value businesses, essentially by comparison to the prices at which other similar businesses or business interests changed hands."[1] Market multiples are:

- **Simple to use.** You can determine them without a lot of calculations. You do not need financial projections three years into the future. You simply need to examine the ratio of a company's revenue and EBITDA to its valuation, as determined by a public company's enterprise value or the price paid for a similar business in a private transaction.

- **Based on real transactions.** There is no guessing about what a business is worth. Shareholders of public companies and buyers in private transactions are rational actors who make informed judgments about how much a company is worth. These determinations influence whether they will buy a company or its stock, and how much they are willing to pay for it.

- **Based on timely information.** The immediacy of the information about market multiples is appealing. When you use market multiples for public companies, the inputs to your valuation were determined the day before, since investors decide what a public company is worth every day the stock market is open. Even the revenue and EBITDA results used in these calculations are current, since regulatory agencies require the disclosure of this information on a regular basis. For private multiples, we consider only those transactions that took place within the last year, to help ensure the data are still relevant. Business owners sometimes fixate on a transaction they heard about several years earlier, but in reality, only recent transactions should be considered because valuation metrics continually change.

Public Versus Private Multiples

In a perfect world, we would rely solely on private transactions when valuing midsize businesses. That is because the companies involved in those transactions are likely to be similar in size to yours. Hence, you are more likely to be comparing apples to apples. As a rule, smaller transactions are valued at lower multiples than larger ones. All else being equal, if a company with $200 million in revenue is sold, it is likely to be sold for lower multiples than a company with $4 billion in revenue. Say, for example, you own a beverage company with $60 million in annual revenue. A quick look at Table 5.1 will give you an indication of which category, public or private, better compares with your company. The median revenue for both sets of comparables is found at Company 8: $4.3 billion for public companies versus $113 million for the private companies. Obviously, multiples of the latter are going to tell you more about your company.

But there's a problem. Accurate valuation requires timely information. For the results to be statistically meaningful, QuickValue requires *15 comparables in the same month*. Yet private transactions involving companies in your industry are likely to occur only periodically. Moreover, we need three pieces of information from each private company transaction: enterprise value, revenue, and EBITDA. Finding all three for a given transaction may be a challenge since with private companies some of this information may go unreported. Exploring a given deal, you might find the purchase price, but not revenue or EBITDA.

For timely answers, we need to look to the realm of public companies. While our revenue figure showed the advantage of using private companies, Figure 5.1 shows just how timely the

TABLE 5.1   Revenue Comparison of Public and
Private Beverage Production Companies

Public Companies	Revenue ($ millions)		Private Companies	Revenue ($ millions)
Pepsico	68,632		Fairlife	500
Coca-Cola	33,463		The Coffee Bean & Tea Leaf	313
Mondelez	25,882		Cytosport	300
Starbucks	24,042		Hojeij Brands	289
Keurig Dr. Pepper	11,277		Morinda Holdings	240
Molson Coors	9,921		Barcelona Wine Bar	128
Treehouse Foods	4,324		Dogfish Head Craft Brewery	115
Monster Beverage	4,304	*MEDIAN*	Montchevre	113
Cott	2,143		Old Orchard Brands	103
Boston Beer Company	1,059		Castle Brands	95
MGP Ingredients	376		Jamba Juice	78
New Age Beverages	256		Cameron's Coffee	72
Celsius Holdings	103		Mountain Valley Spring Co.	50
Alkaline Water Company	45		Senomyx	26
Reed's	36		Ss Brewtech	20

Source: PitchBook, March 2020.

information from public companies can be. As you can see, all 15 public companies are valued in a single month, December, whereas the private company transactions occur throughout the year.

So, public companies solve our timing problem. Yet as mentioned above, the disparity in revenue size creates its own valuation challenges that we must mitigate to come away with reliable results. This is where private transactions come in, albeit

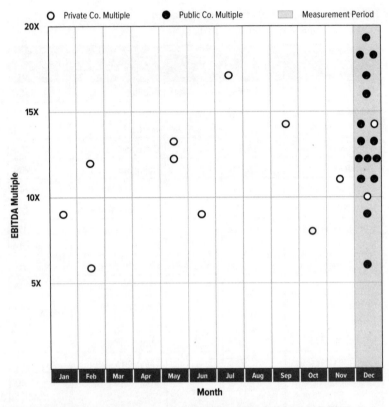

FIGURE 5.1   Timing of public and private company EBITDA multiples.

in a reduced but still essential role. We will use results from private transactions to mitigate the differences between valuations of public companies and private companies closer to your size.

A Range of Values Versus a Single Median

There is another crucial way in which QuickValue differs from traditional valuation methods. Most practitioners who analyze multiples for an industry use the median of the entire group as the standard value. Medians are attractive because they are relatively easy to calculate, and once determined, they offer a clear and handy benchmark of comparison for whatever company you are valuing. Companies in one industry might have a median value of 12x EBITDA, whereas another industry might trade at 15x. Moreover, medians work better than averages. Say, for example, you have 15 multiples from companies in a given industry, ranked 1 through 15. Adding all the multiples and dividing by 15 gives you the average. But averages can be misleading. A single company with extraordinarily high or low performance can give you a false impression of the entire industry. Medians, by contrast, find the midpoint among the 15 companies.

Unfortunately, medians can also be misleading if applied too broadly. Using a single number to describe an entire industry implies, in essence, that all companies in that industry are valued at the same multiple. Whether they are fast-growing innovators with a slew of patents or legacy firms stuck in the doldrums, every company gets painted with the same brush.

In search of more accurate results, QuickValue uses a *range of values* instead of a single overarching median. We do this by calculating medians for the top and bottom halves of an industry's multiples. Don't worry—in the end, we are still going to arrive at a single number representing your company's value. See Figure 5.2 to get a better idea of why taking a little extra time and performing a few more calculations can pay off with a more accurate result. It shows the medians for 10 broad business sectors, breaking out the medians for the top half of performers versus the bottom. In each case, the single median underrates the good performers while overrating the laggards. Consider tech-

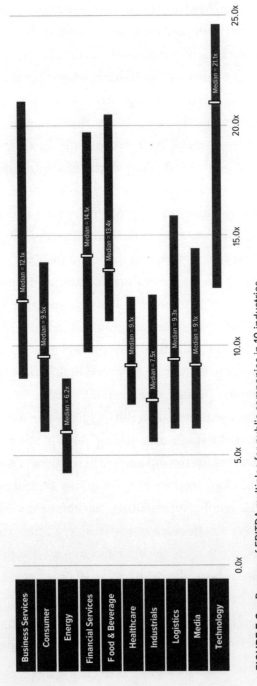

FIGURE 5.2 Ranges of EBITDA multiples for public companies in 10 industries.
(*PitchBook*, February 28, 2020.)

nology. A valuation based on a single median would imply that all technology companies warrant a valuation in the neighborhood of 21.1x EBITDA. Yet the top performers in that industry are worth 24.6x EBITDA—nearly double the 12.6x value for bottom-half performers. By taking into account such disparities, QuickValue offers a more realistic approach.

EBITDA Versus Revenue Multiples

QuickValue's methodology also involves using EBITDA multiples instead of revenue multiples in most cases. When buyers acquire businesses, they usually base their purchase price on the company's EBITDA, not revenue. That is because they are acquiring your firm's profits and adding them to theirs, which will make their company more valuable. Revenue alone, without EBITDA, may not give buyers the boost in value they require. Note that there are some instances in which you will need to use revenue multiples. Early-stage companies or those in hypergrowth mode may have low or even negative EBITDA because the company is reinvesting its profits back into the business to fuel growth. Using EBITDA multiples to determine their value would unfairly penalize them. In some industry sectors, such as software, businesses are valued using multiples of revenue rather than EBITDA. (In Chapter 7, we will spend some time looking at these exceptions and how to handle them.)

Finding Your Industry's Multiples Range

Now that we have covered why QuickValue seeks the information it does, let's get started.

Step 1. Identify Your Industry

The first task is to determine which industry you compete in. While this may sound like a no-brainer, companies often get used to thinking of themselves as part of an industry they *serve*, when, for financial and transaction purposes, they actually belong in a different category altogether. Our Oaklins team in New York recently sold a digital newsletter subscription company, *E&E News*, focusing on energy and the environment. Now, the people in this company knew the energy and environment space inside and out. The industry conferences they attended, the professionals they spoke with and wrote about every day, and the readership they served were all fully immersed in those areas. No wonder, then, that when the time came to value the company for a possible sale, there was some confusion. Not even the owners were sure which industry they belonged in—was it energy and environment, or was it digital subscriptions? While mentally and emotionally they may have counted themselves in the former, for valuation purposes they were solidly in the latter. The company's core function, the driver of its revenue, was producing and selling a newsletter. Prospective buyers later confirmed that assessment. All were media companies that specialized in digital newsletters. In fact, the buyer was POLITICO, a leader in digital news and information.

Even if you know your general industry, you may have to drill down a little further. Within each industry, different types of companies have unique characteristics and multiples. Capital IQ, a prominent service used by investment bankers to track revenue and EBITDA multiples (other services include PitchBook, Bloomberg, and Factset), identifies no fewer than nine industries within the technology sector:

1. Application software—vertical

2. Application software—horizontal

3. Software as a service

4. Data and analytics

5. Infrastructure services

6. Technology hardware

7. IT services

8. Internet

9. Resellers and wholesalers

My Oaklins colleague in Boston, Brad Adams, is an expert in technology deals. He notes that SaaS companies and tech hardware manufacturers, while both belonging to the technology sector, are valued at widely different EBITDA multiples. As shown in Table 5.2, multiples are five times higher for SaaS companies. This divergence illustrates the importance of accurately identifying your industry. Within the nine technology industries, you can dig down still further to find subsets of like companies. For example, a subindustry within infrastructure services is IT security.

TABLE 5.2 Comparison of Technology Multiples

	Technology Industry	
	SaaS	PCs, Servers, etc.
Median Revenue Multiple	10.9x	0.8x
Median EBITDA Multiple	42.1x	8.4x

Source: Hyde Park Capital *Technology M&A Report*, September, 30, 2020.

If you are certain of where you stand, move on to Step 2. If not, start by putting together a list of companies similar to yours. You do not need exact replicas—after all, every company is unique. However, there will be a handful of companies, including direct competitors, that are similar. Think back to the last chapter, when you rated your value drivers. Which names of competitors kept coming up? Don't be afraid to include major corporations. Right now, we are looking for similarities in customers, products, and services. If you participate in an industry trade association, there is probably a group of companies that address the same market as yours does. These companies are good candidates for your list, too. Once you have your list together, examine how those companies describe themselves. Pretty quickly you will see a pattern that defines your industry.

Step 2. Source the Information You Need

Once you have identified your industry, you need to seek out information on public company multiples and private transactions. There are several approaches available to you, depending on your resources, connections, and predilections.

Subscribe to Services. Earlier I mentioned some prominent services that track revenue and EBITDA multiples for publicly traded companies and private transactions. Investment banks and private equity firms are among the most frequent users. You can subscribe directly, but expect an annual subscription of $20,000 or more. This is the simplest method for gaining the multiples you need, but also the most expensive.

The DIY Approach. Finding multiples on your own is less expensive, though it will require a greater investment of time. Public comparables are relatively straightforward. For each company on your list, you will need to know the enterprise value, revenue, and EBITDA. The best free sources that I have found for this information are Yahoo! Finance and Google Finance. Go to the home page and type the name of the public company you are researching into the search box.

Gathering information on private transactions is more involved. Start by checking whether the trade media in your industry compile lists of transactions within the past year, as many do. If you are lucky, they will also offer metrics for revenue and EBITDA multiples. If not, you will need to search each transaction online to see if the information is disclosed. This may feel like panning for gold. You will do a lot of work with only a few good results.

Moving forward, you could also have your finance team keep track of every M&A and financing transaction that occurs in your industry. This is not especially difficult but can be time-consuming. The team will have to routinely read blogs, news releases, and publications about transactions in your industry, and capture the date of the transaction, the enterprise value, the revenue, and the EBITDA. If this information is not made public, your team may need to gather intelligence from lenders, investment bankers, and buyers who considered acquiring the target company but were unsuccessful. (Be sure you trust the source, though, as some may have an ax to grind.) This home-grown approach to information gathering offers some long-term advantages beyond the valuation process, making you and your team that much more aware of the competition and trends in your industry. Yet the commitment involved may not suit every company, and if you are hitting roadblocks, the next source on our list can help.

Ask Your Friendly Investment Banker. A gentle plug here for my compatriots in investment banking. You may have a relationship with an investment banker or know one or two who have contacted you in the past. Ask if, once a year, they will provide you with information you need. More than likely, they will be happy to do so since it will allow them to deepen their relationship with you. They will likely have the stats you need for both public and private multiples. And, importantly, if they are experts on valuations in your industry, they will be able to tell you what the valuation discount is for private transactions when compared with public comparables. This way, you can avoid the calculation.

Some bankers issue regular reports that analyze multiples, so be on the lookout for a banker in your industry that does so (see Appendix 2 for a list of these sources). If you own a SaaS company, you are in luck. Rob Belcher, a managing director at SaaS Capital, a firm that makes loans in the SaaS industry, provides much of what you need at the company's website, www.saas-capital.com. At the end of every month, SaaS Capital provides the median multiple of revenue (SaaS companies are valued using revenue) for B2B SaaS companies. Further, SaaS Capital has determined that the discount factor for private transactions in this industry is 28 percent based on the evaluation of 30 private company valuations. For other industries, you can expect the private company discount to be in the range of 20–35 percent or higher.

We have made some information about publicly traded companies available to you at www.quickvaluemethod.com. Go there, and you will find public multiples for over 100 industries that we obtained through an arrangement with Capital IQ. We will add more over time, but these industries are the ones in which our bankers are most active.

Step 3. Select Public Comparables and Find Median Multiples

Whether you source the information yourself or externally, in the end you need multiples for 15 public companies in your industry. Since not every company will be a perfect fit, you could start with a few more than that, if available, and then narrow your list to the best matches.

As you gather the numbers, be sure to use enterprise value, not market capitalization, because enterprise value more closely approximates a company's true value. Dividing enterprise value by revenue and EBITDA will give you your multiples. For example, a company with an enterprise value of $500 million, revenue of $250 million, and EBITDA of $50 million would have multiples of 2x revenue ($500 million divided by $250 million) and 10x EBITDA ($500 million divided by $50 million).

Let's say you own a bottled water company. Begin by listing every public beverage company you can find that has those multiples available—whether they specialize in water, colas, fruit juices, coffee, or tea. Do not worry if your initial list feels long. Your next job is to narrow and refine the list to get to 15. From that long list, create a new one starting with companies known just for water, since they are clearly the closest to your own. Chances are, though, you will have to add a few more names to get to 15 again. Add in a few names that sell water plus other products, such as colas, juices, and teas. These might include Coca-Cola (Dasani), Pepsi (Aquafina), and Nestlé (Nestlé Waters). If you are still having trouble coming up with 15, expand to companies that specialize in other beverages, but not water.

With your 15 public companies in place, create a grid ranking EBITDA multiples from highest to lowest (see Table 5.3). Essentially, you are creating a mini version of the Dow Jones Industrial Average. Actually, though, since the Dow is based on 30 large-cap public companies representative of the overall market, your list more closely resembles the lesser-known Dow Jones Transportation Average, which tracks 20 public companies in the transportation industry. That is what you are seeking to accomplish for public companies with businesses similar to yours.

TABLE 5.3 Sample Stock Index with EBITDA Multiples
Ranked from Highest to Lowest

		EBITDA Multiple
Company 1		22.7x
Company 2		20.2x
Company 3		19.3x
Company 4		17.6x
Company 5		17.5x
Company 6		17.5x
Company 7		17.3x
Company 8	*MEDIAN*	16.9x
Company 9		15.0x
Company 10		13.7x
Company 11		11.6x
Company 12		10.3x
Company 13		8.8x
Company 14		8.4x
Company 15		7.6x

Once you have created your stock index, determine the median industry EBITDA multiple for the group. When you start with 15 multiples and rank them from highest to lowest, the median is Company 8. After you determine the median, separate the top half of multiples from the bottom in each column, as shown in Table 5.4.

Remove the median (Company 8) from your analysis, so that you have seven multiples (1 through 7) in the top half and seven (9 through 15) in the bottom. Because each half has an odd number of multiples, it is easy once again to find the median for each half. The upper median for the top half is Company 4, and the lower median for the bottom half is Company 12.

TABLE 5.4 Finding Upper and Lower Medians

Public Companies	EBITDA Multiple		Public Companies	EBITDA Multiple	
Company 1	22.7x		Company 9	15.0x	
Company 2	20.2x		Company 10	13.7x	
Company 3	19.3x		Company 11	11.6x	
Company 4	17.6x	*UPPER MEDIAN*	Company 12	10.3x	*LOWER MEDIAN*
Company 5	17.5x		Company 13	8.8x	
Company 6	17.5x		Company 14	8.4x	
Company 7	17.3x		Company 15	7.6x	

Step 4. Account for Public-Private Variances

A key task is to account for the difference in multiples between public and private companies stemming from the fact that public companies are so much bigger. To get there, we will compare the median for public transactions, which is 16.9x EBITDA in Table 5.3, with the median for private transactions, as shown in Table 5.5. Say, for example, nine private transactions occurred in the last 12 months as show in Table 5.5. Your next step is to rank them from highest to lowest multiple and determine the median (Company 5), which is 10.7x EBITDA.

Then compare your median for private transactions with the median for public comparables. In this case, the industry median for public companies is 16.9x EBITDA, and the median for private company transactions is 10.7x EBITDA. Then you simply determine the percentage difference. In this case, private companies are valued at 36.7 percent less than public ones, using the calculation 16.9 minus 10.7, which equals 6.2; and when this is divided by 16.9 and converted to a percentage, you get 36.7 percent.

TABLE 5.5   Sample Industry Index for Nine Private Company Transactions

Private Companies		EBITDA Multiple
Company 1		18.5x
Company 2		14.7x
Company 3		12.2x
Company 4		11.1x
Company 5	*MEDIAN*	10.7x
Company 6		10.3x
Company 7		9.3x
Company 8		7.7x
Company 9		6.9x

Now that we know the variance between private and public multiples is 36.7 percent, we need to adjust our multiples range. Since the multiples range for public comparables is from 10.3x to 17.6x (in Table 5.4), reduce both ends of the range by 36.7 percent. The result is an adjusted EBITDA multiple range of 6.5x to 11.1x, as shown in Table 5.6. This new range accounts for the lower multiples of private transactions.

TABLE 5.6   Private Company Discount for Sample Multiples

	Public Company EBITDA Multiples	Private Company EBITDA Multiples	Private Company Discount
Median	16.9x	10.7x	36.7%
	Public Company EBITDA Multiples	**Apply Private Company Discount**	**Adjusted EBITDA Multiples**
Upper Median	17.6x	36.7%	11.1x
Lower Median	10.3x	36.7%	6.5x

You now have a multiples range for your industry sector that reflects the impact of both public and private comparables, which means you are close to determining your valuation. In the next chapter, we will apply your Value Driver Score to this multiples range to pinpoint your value.

Metrics Mavens and the Search for Multiples

Owner Sylvia had a ball helping the Metrics Mavens QuickValue team develop its value drivers list in Chapter 4. She and Glenn, her sales manager, offered essential perspectives on the company, its products, and its advantages and pain points. But one of her virtues is knowing her limitations. When it comes to finding and calculating multiples, Sylvia takes three steps back. Glenn, the proud non–bean counter, is only too happy to do the same. Now, CFO Joanna and Sarah, the controller, will need to work their magic with EBITDA multiples.

The first step is to fully understand which of three possible industries they belong to: consumer packaged goods, market research, or SaaS. Examining the public companies in each, they rule out SaaS right away. Although they have recurring revenue and use software, they are not a software company in the way that SaaS companies are. And while their customers are in the consumer packaged goods industry, that is not who they are, either. A look at other market research firms confirms that that is where they belong.

With the search field narrowed, they gather multiples for public and private market research companies. Joanna asks Sarah to take charge of that task with her team from the controller's office. Sarah goes to the www.quickvaluemethod.com website and finds her industry included. She is able to get what she needs for the public comparables. Next, she considers the more challenging task of finding information about private companies. She remembers that Jack B., an investment banker who contacts her every so often, always seems to have a handle on how much private market research companies are selling for. An email to Jack yields the answer she is looking for. He tells her that the private company discount for research companies is 20 percent.

Next, Sarah comes forward with her list of EBITDA multiples for public companies, as shown in Table 5.7. The results surprise the members of the team. They had no idea that some companies are valued at almost 28x EBITDA while others are at only 6x. How can they determine what Metrics Mavens' multiple should be? The median value—10.2x (for Company 8)—is a good starting point for their thinking.

TABLE 5.7 EBITDA Multiples for 15 Publicly Held Research Companies

Public Companies		EBITDA Multiple
Company 1		27.5x
Company 2		19.6x
Company 3		16.8x
Company 4	*UPPER MEDIAN*	13.3x
Company 5		13.1x
Company 6		10.9x
Company 7		10.7x
Company 8	*MEDIAN*	10.2x
Company 9		9.3x
Company 10		9.3x
Company 11		9.2x
Company 12	*LOWER MEDIAN*	8.6x
Company 13		7.5x
Company 14		6.1x
Company 15		6.0x

A few more calculations reveal medians for the top and bottom halves of the 15 public company EBITDA multiples— 13.3x (the EBITDA multiple for Company 4) for the top seven companies, and 8.6x (the EBITDA multiple for Company 12) for the bottom seven companies. For the moment, the QuickValue range for Metrics Mavens is therefore anywhere from a high of 13.3x to a low of 8.6x.

But now it is time to fold in the discount for private companies. This will surely lower the range, because in market research, as in most industries, private companies are valued at lower EBITDA multiples than public ones.

Based on the information provided by Jack, the private multiples are 20 percent lower than the public ones. To arrive at an accurate QuickValue range, they now must reduce the multiples from their public company range by 20 percent. These simple calculations (see Table 5.8) bring the central median from 10.2x down to 8.2x, the high median from 13.3x down to 10.6x, and the low median from 8.6x down to 6.9x.

TABLE 5.8 Private Company Discount Applied to Public Market Research Medians

	Public Company EBITDA Multiples	Apply Private Company Discount	Adjusted EBITDA Multiples
Upper Median	13.3x	20%	10.6x
Median	10.2x	20%	8.2x
Lower Median	8.6x	20%	6.9x

Joanna shares the results with Sylvia and the rest of the QuickValue team. As with the value drivers exercise, this multiples analysis on its own offers important information. It reveals the median multiple as 8.2x. That is higher than Martin's offer of 7.5x. But still not close to the number Sylvia's looking for! She thinks her company can be a top-tier player in the industry. The value driver exercise has helped confirm that, and now she is developing the hard numbers to make the case that Metrics Mavens is worth more than the standard rate for private market research firms. In the next chapter, she will put all her findings to the test and, after a few straightforward calculations, find out if she is right.

CHAPTER **6**

Step 3. Calculate Your Value

You are almost there. This stage of the valuation process always takes me back to my days running the 440 for my high school track team, once around the track in an all-out sprint. If you have ever run that particular race, you know the feeling that comes over you about three-quarters of the way around, when your legs turn to jelly, your lungs can't absorb oxygen fast enough, and your whole body begs you to stop. And then, magically, you turn the corner into the last 50 yards, the home stretch. Something about seeing that finish line always gave me a lift. I caught my second wind, gained a step, and finished the race, tired and out of breath but exhilarated by the experience. What I enjoyed most was coming away with a precise time that would tell me not only how I compared with other runners, but whether I was improving over my past times.

So, consider this chapter your home stretch. You have done the heavy work—Chapter 5 in particular may have felt like three-quarters of the way around the track! But now the finish line is in sight. In these last 50 yards, you'll catch a second wind and bring it all together. Using the numbers you generated in previous chapters, you will make a few calculations and come away with a single number representing your company's value. Now keep in mind that valuation, even with the best methods, remains part science and part art. Until the day comes when you actually sell the business, any valuation, no matter how precise, must be considered an approximation rather than an absolute. The ultimate value is what someone else is willing to pay—and you cannot know that until his or her signature is on the contract. What QuickValue gives you is a reliable number against which to evaluate any offer. This can be a potentially powerful negotiating tool. You can back up any case by citing the hard work and mathematics you have undertaken to achieve it. And long before your business goes up for sale, you will have created an essential tool for internal planning, strategy, and growth. As with that high school runner, each time around the QuickValue track will give you a new "best time" to surpass.

Let's briefly review how we got here. In Chapter 3 you selected your QuickValue team and examined your financial statements and accounting methods to make sure they were in order. This was important because we need to use the right results to drive the QuickValue formulas. We reviewed how to add back owner perks and other extraordinary items to determine your adjusted EBITDA—one of the essential numbers in our calculations below. Adjusted EBITDA replicates the true profitability of your business, so we use it in our valuation calculations.

Next came the first step in our three-step calculation process, in which you identified the value drivers most relevant to your business and created a Value Driver Score. In Step 2 you identified your industry and compared your company with others in the same sector. You did this by organizing two sets of comparable multiples, one for public company stocks and another for private company transactions. From the public comparables, you determined the range of EBITDA multiples for your industry sector. Then, to correct for the lower values of midsize versus public companies, you compared the public multiples with the private transaction multiples and made the necessary adjustments.

Now, we are ready for Step 3. This is where your hard work pays off. With just a few more calculations, we will pinpoint the value of your company.

Recall that in Chapters 3, 4, and 5 we created some generic examples showing how to determine your QuickValue essential numbers: adjusted EBITDA, Value Driver Score, and EBITDA multiple range. For consistency, we will use those same results for Step 3:

1. From Chapter 3, adjusted EBITDA: $7.5 million

2. From Chapter 4, Value Driver Score: 30 percent

3. From Chapter 5, EBITDA multiple range: 6.5x to 11.1x

First, for the purposes of our calculations, we need to convert our EBITDA multiple range (6.5x to 11.1x) into a single number. To find the exact multiple, we must calculate the difference between our bottom and top medians. This is easy: Subtracting 6.5x from 11.1x gives us 4.6x. Then apply our Value Driver Score of 30 percent to this amount to find the multiple. Calculating 30 percent of 4.6x gives us 1.4x. This is the amount we add to the bottom median, 6.5x, to find our exact multiple. When we do this, the sum of 6.5x and 1.4x is 7.9x. This is our multiple.

Table 6.1 demonstrates the profound effect Value Driver Scores have on the multiple. A lower score will place our multiple at the low end of the range, closer to the bottom median of 6.5x. As our score increases, the multiple goes up. We can reach the highest point, which is 11.1x, the top median, if our Value Driver Score is 100 percent.

TABLE 6.1   Using Your Value Driver Score to Find Your Multiple

Value Driver Score		EBITDA Multiple
100%		11.1x
90%		10.6x
80%		10.2x
70%		9.7x
60%		9.3x
50%		8.8x
40%		8.3
30%	*YOUR MULTIPLE*	7.9x
20%		7.4x
10%		7.0x
0%		6.5x

Now that we know that our multiple is 7.9x EBITDA, we simply multiply it by our adjusted EBITDA of $7.5 million. Thus 7.9 times $7.5 million gives us the value of the company: $59.3 million.

When you reach this point with your own company, you have gained an important piece of information about your business, one that most owners of midsize companies do not have, and in some cases will never know.

Acting upon this intelligence is what enables you to add even more value to your company. Now that you know which drivers create the most value, you can work to improve the good ones and mitigate the bad ones. You now have a number to use as your benchmark: your value for this year. As you move ahead, you can compare this year's valuation with next year's to measure your performance. Finally, you can use this information to set future goals for your business.

Building a Stronger and More Valuable Company

In the next few chapters, we will examine ways to use this information. In Chapter 7, we look at special situations you may encounter. Sometimes, for example, it is not possible to use EBITDA multiples. Or your business may include multiple product lines, with some in different industries. Or you need to make special adjustments because your business is located in an emerging markets. We have ways to work with each of these scenarios.

In Chapter 8, we will look specifically at how CEOs of portfolio companies owned by private equity firms can use QuickValue. These CEOs are directly rewarded based on value creation, so there is a lot at stake for them in regularly measuring the value of their businesses.

In Chapter 9, we will show how to use your newly determined valuation to further enhance your business. You can incorporate information about your value into your planning, in both the short and long term. This information will immediately inform next year's budget but can also be incorporated in your strategic plan.

In Chapter 10, we will explore ways to use QuickValue to improve your sales process if and when you actually decide to put your business on the market.

Metrics Mavens and the Moment of Truth

With Sylvia waiting excitedly in the wings, Joanna and Sarah pull together all the figures the team has generated thus far. Here is where things stand:

1.   Adjusted EBITDA: $11 million

2.   Value Driver Score: 66 percent

3.   EBITDA multiple range: 6.9x to 10.6x

They are now ready to zero in on the EBITDA multiple for Metrics Mavens:

- First, they take the EBITDA multiple range of 6.9x to 10.6x and subtract the low median from the high median: 10.6x minus 6.9x gives them a spread of 3.7x.

- Next, they apply the Value Driver Score of 66 percent to that 3.7x spread: 66 percent of 3.7x gives them 2.4x.

- Then, they add 2.4x to the low median of 6.9x to arrive at 9.3x. Thus, Metrics Mavens' EBITDA multiple is 9.3x.

- Finally, they apply this multiple of 9.3x to Metrics Mavens' $11 million in adjusted EBITDA: 9.3 times $11 million gives them a clear, defensible value of $102 million for the company.

Recall that Martin S. offered $75 million for the company, based on 7.5x EBITDA (not 9.3x) against $10 million in EBITDA (not $11 million). At the time he made the offer, neither he nor Sylvia was aware of $1 million in add-backs to EBITDA that should be applied. The team only calculated those when preparing the financials for QuickValue (see Chapter 3). But even if Martin were to agree to base his offer on $11 million in EBITDA rather than $10 million, that would still only bring the offer to $82.5 million—$19.8 million short of the company's QuickValue valuation of $102 million. That is because Martin was basing his offer on a multiple of 7.5x rather than the higher multiple of 9.3x the Metrics Mavens team discovered.

When Joanna shares the analysis with Sylvia, the owner breathes a sigh of relief. Had she given in to the temptation to accept Martin's offer on the spot, she might have seriously undersold her company. Martin was not trying to pull a fast one; the offer was made in good faith using the partial information he had available. Still, Sylvia, Joanna, and the rest of the team all agree that Sylvia should ask Martin to consider a counteroffer using the higher EBITDA multiple with the EBITDA add-backs.

By phone the next morning, Sylvia tells Martin she appreciates his interest in the company but feels the offer should be higher. She explains the add-backs to EBITDA and the QuickValue methodology that convinced her the multiple should be 9.3x rather than 7.5x. Martin asks for some time to confer with his team.

The next day, Martin calls back. While he agrees to accept the additional $1 million to EBITDA, automatically increasing the offer from $75 million to $82.5 million, he is willing to go only a little higher on the multiple. While not disputing the figures that brought Sylvia to a multiple of 9.3x, he and his team have determined that Metrics Mavens is only worth 8x EBITDA *to them*. If he had to pay a higher multiple, he explains, his company could create its own version of Metrics Mavens rather than buy hers.

If Sylvia were negotiating out of emotion or gut instinct, she might say yes. After all, $88 million is still an eye-popping figure for a company she developed out of whole cloth just a few years earlier. But the $14 million gap between his new offer and what she now believes to be the true value of her company, based on her team's thorough analysis, seems too much to overlook. Besides, Martin's claim that he can replicate Metrics Mavens feels like a challenge. The Nantucket beach house can wait.

Sylvia and Martin conclude their call with a promise to stay in touch. Meanwhile, Sylvia's competitive juices are flowing as she considers how Metrics Mavens can grow even stronger based on what her team has learned.

PART THREE

USING QUICKVALUE

CHAPTER 7

Special Situations

A central premise—perhaps *the* central premise—behind this book is that there are no "average" companies. QuickValue is designed not just to accommodate but also to celebrate the qualities and characteristics that make your business unique. In fact, your differences—from the way you design your products, to your culture, to the markets you serve—are essential to determining your company's unique value. The process is therefore flexible enough for most midsize businesses in any industry to use as described in the preceding chapters. Yet there are some situations that may require some adjustments. Say, for example, your company has business or product lines in more than one industry. Or you are in an industry where businesses are valued on revenue instead of EBITDA. Or maybe you are a young company or have gone through an unprofitable stretch and have no current EBITDA to speak of. Still others may be located in countries whose emerging economies demand special consideration when it comes to valuing companies.

Never fear. With a few adjustments, you can still arrive at an accurate valuation. In this chapter, we will walk through some of those special situations and how to adjust your calculations.

Your Business Is Involved in More Than One Industry

Your grandfather may have launched the family contracting business in the 1940s, but in the last decade you have been making almost as much money manufacturing and marketing specialized tools for other contractors to use. Or you made your mark as a brick-and-mortar retailer, but now your digital presence has taken off to the point that physical stores may soon be an afterthought. Grouping all your operations into a single category and comparing yourself with a single set of multiples could give you an inaccurate valuation because each side of your business has different growth characteristics and has different competitors to measure yourself against.

Today, many legacy businesses also have digital operations. The two business lines—legacy and digital—must each be valued separately. We are not talking about simply having a website; the need to value separately arises when the digital operation comes to represent a whole new way of doing business. In many cases, the legacy business may be slowing while the digital one is scaling upward. Take a look at the evolution of Netflix. In 1997, the company sold subscriptions to DVDs delivered by mail in those famous red envelopes. Ten years later, Netflix introduced its streaming business, delivering content straight to digital devices. While that business grew, Netflix continued to offer its snail mail delivery to legacy customers still attached to their DVD players.

In 2010, Netflix's DVD rental business had 20 million subscribers. The DVD and streaming businesses have coexisted ever since, but today the DVD business operates at a separate website with its own management team and is dwarfed by the streaming business. As The Motley Fool noted in 2019: "You might think Netflix would have phased out the DVD rental service over the 12 years since it launched its popular streaming service in 2007. However, Netflix has kept the DVD rental business going, and it's still profitable," with 2.7 million subscribers.[1]

In 2013, Netflix added a third business. Not satisfied just to deliver other companies' content, Netflix introduced an original series, *House of Cards*. Its success and that of subsequent productions have shot Netflix to the top of the heap in the content world. Thus, if you were valuing Netflix today, you would do so in three parts: streaming, content production, and DVD-by-mail. You would expect the streaming business to be the most valuable and fastest growing, whereas DVD-by-mail, while still profitable, would be declining and be the least valuable. Each of these businesses has different models, margins, costs, and growth rates and hence deserves different multiples, so the only way to accurately value Netflix is by doing separate valuations for each business.

Midsize businesses with similarly divergent lines should do the same. I recently advised a $115 million company with three primary business lines: magazines, events, and consulting. To understand the company's true value and properly advise its management on strategy, we dove into the financial results and value drivers for each of these three businesses separately.

The magazine business, like most in that industry, was steadily declining. In the space of five years, magazines had gone from being the company's most profitable business to its least, with an EBITDA margin that had eroded to less than 5 percent. The comparatively new events business was growing nicely and lived in an industry with high multiples. Though the events business was much smaller—only $15 million in revenue compared with $85 million for magazines—it had eclipsed magazines in value. Thanks to the higher multiples, it was worth $60 million compared with only $8 million for magazines. The third business, consulting, was also smaller but still worth more than magazines. In Table 7.1, magazines are valued at only 4x EBITDA, compared with 8x for consulting and 12x for events. For the entire company, the EBITDA multiple is 9.2x.

TABLE 7.1 Valuing Multiple Business in the Same Company

	Business Lines			
	Magazines	Events	Consulting	Entire Company
Revenue ($ millions)	$85	$15	$15	$115
EBITDA ($ millions)	$2	$5	$3	$10
EBITDA Multiple	4x	12x	8x	9.2x
Valuation	$8	$60	$24	$92

Had we not taken the time to assess these business lines individually, we might have come away with a markedly different and misleading value for the company. Consider that despite the evolution of their industry, the owners still thought of themselves fundamentally as being in the magazine business—understandable since that represented all their history and most of the revenue. But if we had measured the entire operation according to the magazine industry's 4x multiple, we would have arrived at $40 million, undervaluing the total company by $52 million. By the same token, measuring the whole company by the 12x multiple of its events operation would overinflate the value by $28 million.

Analyzing divergent businesses separately is also essential when it comes to setting your business strategy—a subject we will examine in greater detail in Chapter 9. Without looking at their businesses individually, the owners might have concluded that their still-profitable company was doing just fine and not in need of a makeover. For years, they had remained steadfastly committed to the idea that magazines came first. They had endlessly explored ways to improve the EBITDA margins for magazines by reducing costs and increasing prices—convinced that a few tweaks could turn things around for their central business. While cost reductions were certainly in order, the owners had been blinding themselves to the reality that the magazine business was no longer self-sufficient.

These new insights finally set off the alarm bells. EBITDA from events was worth three times as much and consulting was worth twice as much as EBITDA from magazines. The best path forward, clearly and undeniably, was to build events and consulting and either milk the magazine business for profits or divest it. Had they undertaken regular self-reviews all along, they would have seen much earlier how value was shifting from one year to the next and gotten that much further ahead in their necessary transformation as a company.

That said, you do not need to prepare independent valuations for businesses or product lines that represent only a tiny fraction of your operations. It is important to know where to draw the line. Small parts should be lumped in with larger parts as you prepare your financial statements, as shown in Chapter 3. For example, if three of your businesses each represent 31 percent of revenue and a fourth represents just 7 percent, you can probably bypass a separate valuation for the fourth. That may be too small to bother with, unless it represents a substantial part of your overall value because either it is so profitable or multiples for its industry are so high.

The formal description in the valuation industry for valuing several businesses within the same company is a "sum of the parts" analysis. To perform this analysis, you need separate income statements for each business, and each should calculate profits down to EBITDA. Many companies only calculate EBITDA for the entire business and show "contribution" for individual product lines. Contribution comes after subtracting direct costs from revenue and highlights how your cost per unit compares with revenue. What are missing are fixed costs, such as general and administrative expenses. It would be a mistake not to allocate these costs across each of the business lines. A proper valuation of any business should be based on EBITDA, not contribution.

The additional time and effort you invest in repeating QuickValue for individual business lines will be rewarded by a more precise valuation. And if you decide to sell your company (a subject we'll discuss in Chapter 10), this knowledge may help you attain maximum value—including, potentially, by selling parts to different buyers. Maarten Wolleswinkel, executive chairman of the Oaklins team in Amsterdam, recalled an owner who was disappointed after receiving an offer of 5x EBITDA for his profitable horticulture business. A closer look at the company revealed that under the broad umbrella of "horticulture" were two markedly different operations: a service division that conducted laboratory testing and a chemical division devoted to extending the vase life of flowers. The 5x EBITDA offer came from a buyer in the testing business who was not properly valuing the higher-valued chemical operation. The owner ultimately sold the divisions to different buyers for three times the original offer. And had he chosen *not* to sell, he was armed with valuable insight into how best to invest in growth.

Your Business Lacks Positive EBITDA

EBITDA is the best benchmark for assessing your value. When buyers evaluate businesses, they almost always use EBITDA, not revenue or net income, as the primary determinant of value. But there is a hitch. The "E"—for "earnings"—may not always be there. It could be that you have struggled lately, or unusual events created a temporary hiccup in your string of otherwise profitable years. If your company does not have positive EBITDA in a given year, you don't have to abandon valuation. In fact, it may be more important than ever to understand what's going on. You can default to using revenue as your valuation metric.

Early-stage companies often fall into this category because they're growing rapidly and redeploying excess cash back into the business. This growth naturally understates their profits. Say, for example, you own a fast-growing company with $20 million in revenue. But you are reinvesting all your cash in growth and have no EBITDA. To value the business this year, you should use a revenue multiple. Even next year, when you expect to double revenue and achieve profitability for the first time, EBITDA may still be low enough that the revenue multiple remains the best model.

For QuickValue purposes, revenue multiples work the same way as EBITDA multiples. Simply substitute the EBITDA multiples for both public companies and private transaction comparables with ones for revenue. The rest of the calculations are done exactly as outlined in Chapters 4, 5, and 6.

EBITDA Fluctuates from Year to Year

Some companies by their nature will have inconsistent EBITDA levels from one year to the next. Think of hits-driven businesses such as producers of movies, a TV series, or other entertainment. Your fortunes go up and down with each new release, depending on whether your sizable investment in script, stars, and production resulted in a blockbuster or a flop. Some years may bring several of each, thus distorting your EBITDA for that year. To give an accurate reflection, you will need to correct for the ups and downs by using a two- or three-year moving average.

Other companies may be more predictable in their fluctuations. I once worked with an events company that held its largest event every other year. In off years, its EBITDA was half of what it would be in the years when the event was held. So, averaging EBITDA across two years was an obvious way to arrive at an EBITDA reflective of the value of the company. Likewise, my friend Hugh Roome, president of several divisions at Scholastic Inc., graciously gave my kids a tour of the company when the Harry Potter books were the rage. He told us how the company's profits would skyrocket in years when it released a new book in the series. A midsize business in a similar situation might extend its average EBITDA to two or three years, or however many would reflect both the outsized and more normal years.

Your Industry Is Typically Valued on Revenue Instead of EBITDA

A few industries favor revenue over EBITDA for valuations. The most obvious of these is software as a service. According to investment firm SaaS Capital, which specializes in this industry, profits simply can't keep up with the torrid pace at which these companies are growing. With SaaS businesses, sales and marketing costs are recognized when incurred, while revenue and EBITDA lag. While new customers take time to generate profits, a company is burdened immediately by the costs of obtaining those customers. Later, as those initial costs subside, both the revenue and EBITDA increase as the business grows. The logic goes like this: The only way for most SaaS businesses to become immediately profitable would be to stall growth. As SaaS Capital notes in a white paper, " . . . even for the largest SaaS businesses today, there is little relationship between overall profitability and valuation."[2]

Thus, SaaS companies are valued on their annual run rate (ARR), which works like this: Instead of using the company's preceding 12 months of revenue, you use the current month's and multiply it by 12, thereby annualizing it. If your current month's revenue is $1 million, your ARR revenue is $12 million—despite the fact that your revenue for the trailing 12 months may be substantially lower. This aggressive approach to valuing SaaS companies explains why so many owners and CEOs in other industries have SaaS envy!

Thus, when you are using QuickValue to assess a SaaS company, you simply use the current month's revenue and multiply by 12 to give the effect of a full year. You will do this work in Chapter 3 as you prepare your financial information.

Your Business Is Based in an Emerging Markets Country

Businesses that are not located in the United States or another large, developed economy may need to adjust for some factors to help ensure the accuracy of their valuations. The main challenge may be finding enough domestically based public companies in your industry. Remember, for QuickValue you need 15. If you have fewer, you will need to use ones available from other countries—likely from major economies, which would be countries such as the United States, Germany, and the United Kingdom. But these multiples are likely to be less applicable for companies in your country. In most cases, multiples in emerging economies are lower than those in major economies because the growth opportunities tend to be more limited.

My Oaklins colleagues in Buenos Aires, Alejandro Dillon, Julian Emiliozzi, and Lucrecia Granda, have developed an ingenious solution for this problem. They adjust the multiples to correspond with the Argentine market by comparing their country's stock index, the S&P MERVAL, with stock indexes of the countries from which a company originates. "We adjust the stock index multiples to take into account macroeconomic, political, and regulatory issues and other differences between

Argentina and the economy where the public company is located," Dillon says.

Two years ago, the three were valuing an Argentine company in the flexible packaging industry. When they searched that industry for public company comparables, they found just 13 globally. That is 2 fewer than the 15 I suggest for QuickValue, but a workable number for emerging markets, according toDillon. None were in Argentina; the companies were in the United States, Australia, China, Taiwan, Canada, South Africa, Chile, Colombia, and Brazil. Table 7.2 shows how the stock indexes for each of these countries differ from the S&P MERVAL and what discount should be applied to make them comparable.

TABLE 7.2 Country Stock Indexes Compared with Argentina's MERVAL

Country	Stock Index	Average EBITDA Multiple	Discount to the MERVAL
Argentina	MERVAL	6.1x	0%
United States	S&P 500	12.4x	−51%
Canada	S&P/TSX Composite	10.7x	-43%
South Africa	Johannesburg	9.9x	−39%
Brazil	BOVESPA	8.2x	−26%
Colombia	Bolsa de Valdores	10.3x	−41%
Taiwan	Taiwan TAIEX	8.6x	−30%
China	Shanghai	11.9x	−49%
Australia	Australian	15.3x	−60%
Chile	Bolsa de Santiago	8.6x	−30%

Source: Oaklins team in Argentina, 2018.

Now that we know how much to discount stocks in other economies to make them correspond with the Argentine market, we apply the discount to the stocks in Table 7.3. This allows us to create a stock index for companies in the flexible packag-

TABLE 7.3 Public Company Flexible Packaging Multiples as Adjusted for Argentina's MERVAL

Company	Country	EBITDA Multiples	Discount to the MERVAL	Adjusted EBITDA Multiples
Amcor plc	Australia	13.5x	−60%	5.4x
Berry Global Group, Inc.	United States	9.1x	-51%	4.4x
Carvajal Empaques S.A.	Colombia	9.2x	−41%	5.4x
Crown Holdings, Inc.	United States	10.0x	−51%	4.9x
Envases del Pacifico S.A.	Chile	8.0x	−30%	5.6x
Intertape Polymer Group Inc.	Canada	9.9x	−43%	5.6x
Nampak Limited	South Africa	5.6x	−39%	3.4x
Sealed Air Corporation	United States	11.9x	−51%	5.9x
Taiwan Hon Chuan Enterprise Co.	Taiwan	7.1x	−30%	5.0x
Tredegar Corporation	United States	6.9x	-51%	3.4x
Viskase Companies, Inc.	United States	8.4x	−51%	4.1x
Winpak Ltd.	Canada	9.5x	−43%	5.4x
Zhuhai Zhongfu Enterprise Co., Ltd.	China	24.7x	−49%	12.6x

Source: Oaklins team in Argentina, 2018.

ing industry as they would be valued if they were all located in Argentina.

This approach is also relevant for companies that have product lines that are distributed across different geographies. Some may be in major developed economies and others in emerging ones. It would be prudent to value them according to both their geographies and industry sectors, using the method my Oaklins colleagues in Argentina have created. The numbers are readily and publicly available, and your financial team should be able to pull them together fairly quickly.

These are the major variables that could warrant a few extra or different steps in your valuation process. You are now armed with several ways to use QuickValue when you encounter unusual situations. We will be continually updating our information, so please visit www.quickvaluemethod.com for the latest. And if you come across your own unusual situation not covered here, let us know, and we will consider adding that to the list. Because QuickValue is intended as an annual process, we will continue looking for ways to make it work better for you each time you do a valuation.

In the next chapter, we will explore another special situation: private equity ownership. The CEOs of these companies have unique challenges where QuickValue can be useful.

CHAPTER 8

Private Equity CEOs

In this chapter, we are going to look at a specialized and growing category of midsize businesses—those owned by private equity investors. The challenges they face differ from those of traditional companies in that the imperative to produce results is compressed and intensified. The average life span for a private equity investment is three to five years. In that short time, the business must improve and grow—in other words, increase in value—to achieve the financial return that investors expect. This requires the owners to be hyperfocused on value creation. As we will see, the private equity firms that invest in these companies have their own tried-and-true approaches to valuation. Yet the CEOs and executives who manage the companies and are charged with growing them also have a deep interest in understanding and measuring the value they are creating. That knowledge can be essential in helping them fulfill their mission to the benefit of the company and themselves. If you serve as a CEO or manager for such a company, QuickValue can help you better understand the value you are creating for the company and for yourself and help put you on an even footing when you meet with your owners to discuss progress toward your goals.

What Private Equity Owners Want

Private equity firms raise capital based on the idea that they can acquire companies, improve them, and sell them again for a nice financial gain. They hedge their risk by creating a fund to acquire perhaps 8 or 10 companies with the idea that some will be tremendously successful and make up for others that underperform. This is similar to a private investor's stock portfolio, except that instead of owning a small stake in a public company, private equity firms own all or most of the private companies they invest in.

The process starts with an investment thesis for each company. Larry Jones, of Aegis Management LLC, has worked with several private equity firms as a CEO, operating partner, and board member. He says typical objectives include growing revenue, gross margins, and EBITDA and conserving cash to pay down bank debt. The firms may also seek to increase revenue streams that create greater value, reduce lower-value ones, grow or shift the client base, or even acquire other companies. And private equity firms tend to be pragmatic and unsentimental about making adjustments. According to an article by *Strategy&*, "Private equity firms make it their business to understand how each activity contributes to value creation and diligently cut costs on low-value activities. That can often mean exiting entire lines of business that are simply not drawing on the company's core strengths."[1]

The investors who put most of the capital into private equity funds are called limited partners, which means their roles are largely passive. They look to the investment executives who create the funds to oversee each investment, including working with competent, motivated CEOs and managers and taking board positions at each of their portfolio companies. The investment executives, in turn, look to these CEOs and managers for regular updates on how the companies are performing.

Private equity firms are required to mark the value of their portfolios to market every quarter. Even without this requirement, most would be doing so anyway. Their investors expect it, and even more important, measuring value creation is central to their success. High expectations and careful monitoring produce results. In data published by the National Center for the Middle Market, midsize companies owned by private equity generated revenue growth of 9.09 percent a year compared with 6.32 percent for other midsize companies.[2] That's 44 percent better, which is meaningful.

How Private Equity Tracks Value Creation

Because the time period in which they own a company is so compressed, most private equity firms value their portfolios as often as quarterly. Some look to investment bankers who specialize in the industries in which their portfolio companies operate. They also run their own valuation models. "We are very rigorous in keeping tabs on value," says Peggy Koenig, chair of ABRY Partners, a Boston-based fund with $12.8 billion under management. "We do a detailed valuation every quarter, and twice a year we present the results to our advisory boards for approval." (Private equity companies, it should be noted, have the resources to conduct frequent valuations and an obligation to their shareholders. Independent companies do not need to that frequently. Yet the emphasis that private equity places on valuation offers a good illustration of why *any* company should conduct valuations yearly.)

Great Hill Partners almost always relies on public and private comparables for its valuations, notes Chris Gaffney, cofounder and managing partner. Only in rare exceptions will the firm use the discounted cash flow method. Recently, when one of Gaffney's 33 portfolio companies faced serious disruption related to the coronavirus pandemic, Great Hill Partners switched to DCF because current revenue and EBITDA were artificially depressed. Generally, though, Gaffney believes the DCF method is too easy to manipulate because it is based on myriad assumptions that can be changed to get the valuation you want. When Great Hill examines comparables to develop its valuations, the availability of private comparables varies widely. "In some instances," says Gaffney, "the list is a mile long. In others we might only find one good comparable." To find M&A comparables, the firm uses a combination of industry databases and conversations with investment bankers active in their portfolio company's industry.

As a rule, valuations by private equity firms tend to be conservative compared with what the company might actually bring in a sale. That is no accident. When companies in a portfolio ultimately sell for more than they were valued at, that "lift" (as it is known in the industry) creates a happy surprise for limited partners. When the portfolio companies sell for less, firms can expect the opposite reaction. "You never want to surprise your limited partners by overvaluing a portfolio company," Gaffney says. To prove his point, he says Great Hill's average lift is two times the industry average. Great Hill measures value based on multiples of *trailing* revenue and EBITDA, even though the higher-growth companies are likely to be sold using *forward* revenue and EBITDA figures—which results in higher valuations.

The Valuation Knowledge Gap

Private equity firms select CEOs and managers they believe are capable of swiftly building a company's value, so compensation is naturally tied directly to that goal. The approach has proved to be effective over the years. The interests of management are aligned with those of the investors. Both seek to create as much value as possible since that is how they maximize their individual returns. Thus, CEOs and managers have just as much interest as the private equity firms they work for to track the value of their companies. Larry Jones has served on every side of the private equity landscape, as both an operating partner and CEO of several mid-size companies. "As CEO, I am always tracking my equity value," he says. "To do so, I need to calculate the enterprise's value."

Perhaps surprisingly, given the close working relationship between private equity firms and their portfolio companies' CEOs, that information may not be part of the conversation when the parties gather to discuss progress. "We don't spend a lot of time focusing on an annual valuation in discussions with the CEOs of our portfolio companies," says Peggy Koenig of ABRY Partners. "Instead, we spend time on strategies to create long-term value—growing the customer base, upselling customers, launching new products, expanding geographies, managing expenses, adding to and upgrading the management team, and doing follow-on acquisitions. These initiatives are intended to translate into value creation."

Koenig makes an excellent point, and her firm's record of success proves this assertion. As we discussed in Chapter 4, isolating and focusing on a company's value drivers is critical. Great Hill Partners, likewise, does not make a practice of sharing its valuation results with the portfolio companies, Chris Gaffney says. Those valuations are created mainly for limited partners and, as we have heard, can be conservative. To get the information they desire, CEOs and managers may have to look elsewhere.

For US companies, one marker is the 409A valuation, which assesses a private company's total stock value, much the way market capitalization does for a public company. The IRS requires 409As for any private company offering stock options as compensation. Yet while market capitalization involves relatively simple calculations based on publicly listed stock prices, a 409A requires a more subjective, independent valuation. These valuations (like those generated by private equity firms) tend to be conservative, and may not fully capture the value that the management team is creating. To try to gain a more precise look, "I stay in touch with investment bankers and keep an eye on M&A and capital raising transactions in my industry for revenue and EBITDA multiples," Larry Jones says.

Despite their overall alignment, there are times when the CEO and private equity firm will differ on strategy. From the outset, CEOs prefer to take on less debt and preserve more cash. This, of course, is at odds with the private equity formula of supercharging equity returns by using debt financing. CEOs typically want to use excess cash to invest in acquisitions or support growth initiatives. The private equity team also wants growth, of course, but may prioritize paying a dividend to investors over paying down bank debt.

Some private equity firms may decide to recapitalize their investment in a portfolio company. In other words, after some value has been created, but before an eventual sale, they decide to use more debt from the company to repay all or part of the initial equity investment. Many private equity firms recapitalize because their limited partners expect it. And why not? What could be better than investing in a company and a year or two later getting all your invested capital back—and still owning the company?

This situation recently unfolded for one of our Oaklins clients. We sold 80 percent of the business to a private equity firm and the seller retained 20 percent, a fairly common division of equity between private equity and the management team. Eighteen months later, the private equity firm decided to recapitalize, borrowing enough to pay investors a dividend that would in effect return to them all their equity investment. The firm was now using "house money" to ride out the rest of the investment. This was presented as a win-win to the CEO and management team because they were also getting cash equal to their equity ownership of 20 percent. Yet by taking this course, the private equity firm clearly prioritized hedging its bet and "derisking" its investment, versus using that borrowing capacity for acquisitions or growth capital. This was not what the management team felt it signed up for. When the company was acquired, the team expected to increase the company's value using capital provided by the private equity firm for acquisitions and growth initiatives it could not have made when the company was independent. Recapitalization might be the right use of funds in some cases, but growth opportunities may be sacrificed and the company saddled with significantly more debt. Small wonder that, as the *New York Times* reports, "The practice has a divisive history."[3]

Bridging the Gap

Divisiveness is the last thing you want in a relationship based on deep mutual interests and where both sides play a crucial role in the venture's success. For CEOs and managers, QuickValue can help you gain an even footing in valuation discussions—not to do battle but to help drive communication and strategy and ensure that your unique perspectives on the company are being heard.

When you tell the private equity team you plan to conduct your own valuation, do not be surprised if at first you encounter some skepticism and resistance. After all, this is a space that the private equity team is used to owning outright. Explain your reasoning: Your interest in valuation is based on more than tracking your equity stake. You want the best for the company, for the private equity team, and for the limited partners. The more you understand about valuation, the more you will add to the process, the more productive your conversations will be, and the more you will be able to help when the team makes crucial decisions about capital and growth. Emphasize that the process should be collaborative.

This is how it might work. As CEO, you and your management team should identify and rate the value drivers. You know the business inside and out and are perfectly situated to do this. As we noted earlier, value drivers are already likely to be a key component of your discussions with the private equity team. A proactive approach, undertaking the disciplined process described in Chapter 4, can enrich your insights and help you drive those conversations rather than simply responding to questions. Once a draft is completed, share it with the members of your private equity team for their input, and use it as the basis for a lively discussion around the value drivers you selected, your ratings, and your Value Driver Score.

You can further involve the members of the private equity team by asking them to supply multiples—the building blocks of Chapter 5. They have access to multiples from databases they subscribe to and from their relationships with investment bankers. Once the multiples are gathered, review them together. When everyone agrees on value drivers and multiples, put the pieces together to determine your value, as laid out in Chapter 6. Use the results to debate strategy and set future plans for the business, including questions such as these:

- How much value can be created if excess cash is invested in the business rather than paying down debt?

- What kind of return on investment do we need from an acquisition to prioritize it over investing in the current business?

- Which value drivers are the most important to improve? Which can be improved within the investment horizon of three to five years? What is the financial impact of improving one value driver over another?

- Are buyers rewarding faster growth or higher EBITDA in our industry? Which should we prioritize so that we maximize value?

Your private equity firm will still conduct its own separate valuation for its investors. Yet for internal discussions on strategy and growth, you will have an essential tool to build collaboration, cooperation, and trust. Rather than passively agreeing to ideas presented by the private equity firm, you will be better equipped to challenge those ideas and promote your own.

We will delve further into how QuickValue can be used to guide strategy in the next chapter. We will start by looking at using your QuickValue analysis alongside your annual budget, historical financial statements, strategic plan, and other essential documents. And we will check back in with Sylvia and her Metrics Mavens team as they set out, with a new sense of purpose and excitement, to plan for the years ahead.

CHAPTER 9

Guiding Your Strategy

Thanks to the work you have done so far, you now possess something that puts you in rare company among midsize businesses: a single, defensible, *internally generated* number expressing the current market value of your company. But what if you are not ready to sell? The rewards may be out there someday, but—with apologies to Robert Frost—you have miles to go before you reap. Your QuickValue results are as important as ever. In this case, the star of the show isn't so much the final number you arrived at but the steps you took to get there. They can help guide you as you work to eliminate weaknesses, capitalize on strengths, and find ways to prosper in a hypercompetitive world. In this chapter, we're going to shift our focus from "How much?" to "Why?" So, put that number aside for the time being.

Enjoy it. Take pride in it. Savor it as you drive home after a long day's work. Meanwhile, let's roll up our sleeves and examine how to use the treasure of information your QuickValue analysis has unearthed to help guide your strategy for growth.

Why Strategic Planning Matters

Think of the most important questions facing your business. How much should we be investing in digital operations? Should I resuscitate that lagging business line or divest and focus on more profitable areas? How stable is our revenue? Which competitors represent the greatest threats, and why? Can we scale up to take advantage of a new opportunity? How much should we be pouring into R&D? Do we need to acquire new capabilities? How can I incentivize my management team to grow the business?

Too many midsize companies deal with these types of questions reactively, in response to an unforeseen challenge or emergency. Their planning process, such as it is, may involve little more than creating an annual budget. Budgets are important. Every company needs them. But they are short-term blueprints for the year ahead. They don't say much about where you are headed the year after that and beyond. They do not address the big questions.

For that, the best approach is a more formalized, long-term strategic plan. Strategic plans, like traditional valuations, can be complicated and time-consuming to pull together, which is one reason that too few midsize companies undertake them. And there are many different ways to go about it. That is a subject for another book. But with a little work, you can find an approach that works well for your company, is relatively straightforward and cost efficient, and yet is detailed and complete enough to serve your needs. Two of the best books on the subject are John Doerr's *Measure What Matters: How Google, Bono, and the Gates Foundation Rock the World with OKRs*, published in 2018, and *Good Strategy Bad Strategy: The Difference and Why It Matters*, by Richard Rumelt. Doerr, one of Silicon Valley's most successful venture capitalists, recommends a close review of "objectives and key results" (OKRs) as a simplified and powerful approach to strategic planning. Rumelt's book was published in 2011, but his advice on how to select the right strategy is still relevant today.

First, let's review some of the fundamentals of any strategic plan and how your QuickValue findings can make your plan better, stronger, and more dynamic. After that, we will look at how to guide your strategy—even if you are not doing formal planning on a regular basis—by creating a series of "mini plans" based on your value drivers.

Your Strategic Plan

As the Corporate Finance Institute notes, strategic planning involves three basic steps: formulation, implementation, and evaluation. Step 1, formulation, involves assessing your current situation, including your strengths, weaknesses, opportunities, and threats, as well as a statement outlining your company's mission and goals. In Step 2, implementation, you create a plan for pursuing those goals and fulfilling your mission. The final step involves evaluating your performance and taking corrective action where you are falling short.

Recall that in Chapter 4, you applied the SWOT analysis to rate your most important value drivers on your way to calculating your Value Driver Score. Here, we will take that process a step further, using SWOT and your value drivers to plan for the future. Your 8 to 12 value drivers are the ones that you and your team identified, through vigorous debate and a careful process of elimination, as the qualities most important to your business. They represent your greatest strengths, the weaknesses you most need to work on, the opportunities you should work hardest to capture, and the threats you need to protect against. Having already gone through that process, you have a big head start on one of the most important aspects of strategic planning.

A good rule of thumb is to recognize what you can and cannot control. When it comes to your finances, for example, your actions can directly influence your revenue and EBITDA. But nothing you do is going to alter the multiples being paid for companies in your industry. The same holds for value drivers. Some of the value drivers on your list may be largely or entirely out of your control. You cannot, for example, control the barriers to entry for your industry (value driver 8). Nor can you do a whole lot to change your industry's overall market size and potential value (value driver 1), the market trends in your industry (value driver 2), or the level of competition you face (value driver 14). While these may be essential to determining your value and thus warrant a place on your list, they may play a lesser role in your strategic plan.

For strategic planning purposes, you will want to give added emphasis to qualities you can directly build and improve on. You can take direct steps to modify your business premise (value driver 3), improve your culture (value driver 12), and ramp up the level of innovations (value driver 15). These are the ones where you have a runway to make tangible improvements.

Strengths and Weaknesses

Dividing your value drivers into those you can control and those you cannot will immediately produce insights for your business strategy. If your poorest-rated value drivers—your weaknesses—are within your control, this is good news. You can introduce changes to improve your scores. In a moment, we will talk about ways to create mini plans for these areas. If, on the other hand, your worst-performing value drivers (those you rated below 4) are clustered on the list and are ones beyond your control, that could be an indication you need to rethink the business you are in. What your value drivers may be telling you is that you have limited ability to improve your business and are subject to the whims of external forces. We will view these as potential threats to the long-term viability of your business.

What if the opposite is true? All your highest-rated value drivers—your strengths—fall into the category of things you can control. Your product quality is rocking, your customers love the way you treat them, and your revenue is consistent and growing steadily. Though that is strong evidence of a well-run company, it also poses a challenge. With less room to move the needle on things you are already great at, it may be time to explore new avenues to grow the value of your business.

Chances are that like most midsize companies you fall somewhere between those extremes. Among the value drivers you can control are some you excel at and others that need work. For each, you will want to create an action plan. For highly rated value drivers, your plan will likely focus on doing whatever is needed to preserve your rating. For low-scoring value drivers, you will need a turnaround plan.

Yet keep in mind that no value driver stands alone. Value drivers overlap and influence one another. Consider pricing power (value driver 19). Early in my career, when I worked in magazine publishing at *The New Republic*, we knew that pricing was one of our weaknesses. We had a dedicated readership of 100,000, and the quality of the magazine's editorial content was unsurpassed. Yet at the time I arrived, a yearly subscription (48 issues) went for $24, while other popular weeklies, such as *People* and *The Economist*, commanded nearly $100.

The conventional wisdom among businesses was to incrementally test pricing power before making substantial increases. In my first year we increased the subscription price to $28, after testing price points between $26 and $29. That was a good start, but based on the chasm between our rates and those of other magazines, we knew we still had room to grow.

We decided to strategize pricing power in tandem with another value driver that we had control over and that needed substantial improvement: customer experience (value driver 31). The problem was not editorial content—as I said, that was top-notch. The problem was getting the magazine into the hands of all readers in a timely fashion. This was back in the days when subscribers read their magazines exclusively in print editions delivered by the US mail. Our copies were printed every Thursday evening at a plant near our Washington, DC, offices. While East Coast subscribers received their magazines within a few days, some as early as Saturday, those west of the Mississippi River might not get theirs for a week. Even in the predigital age, that was a long time to wait for our writers' perspectives on rapidly changing political events.

We addressed this problem with some simple but effective fixes. Instead of sending copies directly to the post office for sorting, as we had done in the past, we started sorting by region at our printer's plant. We sent presorted bins straight to the train station next to the main post office, where copies of the latest issue were loaded directly onto trains headed for various destinations. Eliminating the postal service sorting process meant that subscribers in California received their copies on Mondays instead of Thursdays. West Coast readers were now reading the magazine only days after the articles were written.

A year after these changes, and with marked improvement in customer experience, we raised our subscription prices by 29 percent, to $36. The next year we bumped the price another 25 percent, to $45. These were the most aggressive price increases in the history of the magazine and might have seemed reckless if we had enacted them in an arbitrary bid for higher revenue. After all, a standard rule of thumb holds that a price increase of 5 percent will cause sales to decline by 5 percent. Yet we found that for every 5 percent price increase, we lost less than 0.5 percent of our subscribers. That meant the trade-off was well worth it. The reward was more revenue from subscribers and greater profits for the business. Our decisions were not arbitrary in the least. Rather, they were part of a concerted strategic effort to improve two of our essential value drivers, thus converting weaknesses into strengths.

Opportunities

One of the greatest opportunities for midsize businesses lies in the ability to raise capital for expansion. Unlike their public company counterparts, though, they cannot simply issue more stock. Options include raising debt or growth capital.

In 2004, we were hired by two brothers, Michael Kong and Stephen Kong, whose business of publishing high-end luxury magazines in major cities was growing nicely. They had started in Chicago and expanded to Los Angeles and Dallas. Their formula was working well, and they saw the opportunity to grow even faster. Instead of starting one new magazine each year, they believed they could start three, but they needed investment capital to do so. We were tasked with finding a minority investor who would acquire an equity stake of less than 50 percent and allow the brothers to get a nice payday and growth capital for their expansion. My Oaklins partner, Roland DeSilva, arranged for the brothers to partner with Shamrock Capital, a private equity fund started by Roy Disney and specializing in media. Thanks to that successful relationship, the brothers were able to expand quickly to many more cities. A few years later, they sold the company for more than six times what it had been valued at prior to the partnership.

That case illustrates the power that a strategic injection of capital at the right time can have in terms of taking a promising company to the next level. But access to that capital requires convincing investors and lenders that the money they invest or lend will generate future profits and value.

Through your QuickValue analysis, you have credible documents demonstrating not just your value but the reasons behind it—the *why*. Investors and lenders will be impressed. This is the kind of information they are accustomed to determining on their own by examining a prospective client's financial statements. Though they will certainly conduct their own valuations before committing, sharing your QuickValue results will tell them a lot. You will reveal underlying strengths they might have missed and demonstrate how you are already working to correct and improve any weaknesses. Beyond that, you will demonstrate a reassuring self-awareness of what your business is about and where you want to take it, and will show you are a good partner, committed to transparency. Investors and lenders, at heart, are looking to be a part of your success story because that is why they do what they do. But first they need to be convinced that you understand that story better than anyone else and are not just making it up as you go along. QuickValue can provide the central building blocks for your narrative.

Threats

Hardly any business is immune to disruption. To make the right decisions about your strategy, you need to know how the value of your business is changing as disrupters flex their muscles and make inroads in your industry.

History is replete with once-dominant companies that ignored this lesson. Among the most obvious examples are Kodak and Blockbuster. In the mid-1970s, when Kodak sold 90 percent of the film and 85 percent of the cameras in the United States, one of its engineers invented the first digital camera. Kodak famously decided to double down on old-fashioned film and traditional cameras while other companies seized the digital opportunities. By 2012, Kodak was declaring bankruptcy. In 2004, Blockbuster, the biggest player in video rentals, was at its peak with 9,094 retail stores. Four years earlier, entrepreneurs Reed Hastings and Marc Randolph offered Blockbuster the opportunity to buy their upstart business, Netflix, for $50 million.[1] Blockbuster declined. By 2010, the video giant was filing for bankruptcy, and Netflix was the largest source of evening internet streaming traffic in North America.

Yet those cautionary tales are balanced by other stories in which companies recognized threats and turned them into opportunities. By 2010, most traditional media companies had abandoned their once-profitable classified advertising operations, driven out by Craigslist and other digital competitors. The German company Axel Springer adopted a contrarian strategy, diving full force into digital classifieds. Jens Mueffelmann, then the company's chief digital officer, recognized that jobs, homes, and cars—bedrock components of classified advertising—represent some of the most pivotal decisions in a person's life. Customers, he believed, would pay to get access to the best information and options. Axel Springer began acquiring and building digital classified sites for jobs, real estate, and automobiles. In 2012, the company formed a partnership with the private equity firm General Atlantic to fund even faster growth. The business scaled quickly, and by 2016, revenue was €880 million with EBITDA of €355 million. By then, 54 percent of all the EBITDA generated by Axel Springer came from the digital classifieds business, which today is the largest in Europe.

The global coronavirus pandemic, of course, only escalated the pace of change for companies across every industry. Airbnb, for example, saw its core business threatened as travelers suddenly shunned hotels and shared spaces in cities. Noticing that city dwellers were searching for rentals in smaller towns nearby, to escape cities and avoid air travel, the company shifted to focus on travelers seeking local destinations. "I did not know that I would make 10 years' worth of decisions in 10 weeks," CEO Brian Chesky told the *Wall Street Journal*.[2]

Now, QuickValue will not enable you to predict the next global crisis or anticipate every business challenge. But value drivers and other elements of your yearly valuation can help keep you ahead of changes, and, as well, help you understand how they'll affect your business and how you can turn your own threats into opportunities. Keeping an eye on how your value drivers are changing from one year to the next will alert you to threats you need to deal with. Maybe the barriers to entry are eroding for one of your products to the point where that value driver is losing its importance. It could be time to transition to new products.

Using Mini Plans in Place of a Formal Strategic Plan

If formal strategic planning feels like overkill for a company like yours, or you just have not been able to devote the time and resources to creating a plan, QuickValue can fill the gap. The 8 to 12 value drivers you identified in Chapter 4 as essential to your business provide a framework for examining your strengths, weaknesses, opportunities, and threats. You can use that information to create a series of mini plans to drive your company forward.

The mini plan process involves three steps: evaluate, plan, repeat. Having already evaluated, identified, and rated your value drivers in Chapter 4, you can move directly to creating a plan outlining how you will manage each value driver for the next three to five years and specifying the steps you will take to set that plan in motion. Each year, review and repeat the process, looking closely at the progress you have made toward your existing objectives, and, based on your latest QuickValue results, identify new ones you may need to establish.

Begin your process by discussing each value driver, one at a time, with your team. Consider how you rated the individual drivers. For those where you are on a roll, build a plan around how to stay there. Consider a media company whose business model involves signing advertisers to two- or three-year contracts for access to affluent audiences in some of America's wealthiest communities. The steady revenue stream from extended contracts is a big reason that visibility of future revenue (value driver 10) rates as one of the company's most important and successful value drivers. To maintain that high rating, the company knows its advertisers must see results that justify long-term commitments. As part of its mini plan for this value driver, the company establishes a goal of 85 percent positive ratings from advertisers, to be determined from regular surveys. To help improve the experience for dissatisfied advertisers, the sales team commits to strengthen its outreach, sharing information about its audiences and strategizing with advertisers on how to better focus their campaigns.

More important is to dive in on the value drivers where you need the most work, particularly those over which you have the most control. Consider a company that provides paint samples to interior designers. The company has traditionally shipped samples anywhere in the United States, with a six-day delivery schedule. This works well until a new competitor starts providing samples overnight. Suddenly, time to market (value driver 23) becomes an imperative. This company needs a mini plan that examines how it can improve its time to market. Part of its plan would explore the cost implications of delivering samples overnight to match its competitor's strategy.

Treat each value driver independently. What are the strengths, weaknesses, opportunities, and threats contained within that specific value driver? With that mini SWOT analysis complete, identify the actions you should take, and set ambitious but realistic and measurable goals for improvement. For example, if you have identified market share (value driver 17) as a vital area for your company to improve, this is what your mini plan might look like:

Goal: Improve market share.

Objective: Increase market share by five percentage points within three years.

Action Plan:
  1. Spend $5 million on brand awareness advertising.
  2. Reduce prices by 10 percent.

As you can imagine, there is interplay between your plan for this value driver and others. Be aware that spending $5 million on advertising could have a short-term impact on profitability and return on invested capital (value driver 6). And reducing prices might require you to increase your efficiency, thereby affecting your economies of scale (value driver 9). You may need to relax your plans for some value drivers while you seek to improve others.

Ultimately, you may want to transition to a more formal method of yearly strategic planning. Meanwhile, these mini plans covering your most important value drivers will ensure that your company stays headed in the right direction beyond next year's budget.

Creating Incentives for Growth

The process of growing your company and achieving long-term stability requires the total commitment of your team. Top public company executives are rewarded handsomely when company value rises. For public companies, that is easy to quantify by pegging rewards to growth in the stock price.

Private companies can benefit from offering similar incentives, but doing so is more complex. Many reward their management teams for improving revenue or EBITDA. But for all the reasons we discussed in this book, a company's underlying value, whether rising or falling, is the best indication of how that company is doing.

Some private companies reward executives with an ownership stake. That's a good move (one that too few companies opt for, in my opinion) since it gets closer to the idea of incentivizing people for building value. Unfortunately, those executives may only realize significant benefits when the company is sold, which could be years away, or in some cases, never. QuickValue offers you a means to reward value creation on an annual basis, just as public companies do by awarding stock options. During each year that your analysis reveals a growth in value, your team shares in the good news.

Planning for Pleasant Surprises

So far, we have focused on doing everything you can to prepare, plan, and strategize. Yet not all value is created as if manufactured in a lab full of business strategists. Sometimes it happens inadvertently, through happy surprises. A pharmaceutical manufacturer, say, works for years to create a new drug to solve a particular condition. When the drug is ready, tests reveal it is actually the perfect treatment for another condition altogether.

A client I work with provides digital marketing services. As a services business, the client does not have the opportunity to build value through products. What it has built, though, are online communities, which it uses to sell products manufactured by its clients, receiving a fee for each sale. Though that fee-based model drives the business, the client found that it had inadvertently created something with considerable independent value. In addition to the processes and technology and to the revenue and EBITDA generated by its clients' sales, there is the hidden gem of the communities it has created. The right buyer will be able to mine these relationships and expand the offerings to this valuable, built-in audience.

Your company may be building unexpected value in some similar fashion. The better you are at recognizing this serendipity, the more likely it is that you will be able to fully exploit its potential for growth. Each year consider how your value drivers are changing. If some are forcing their way onto the list, or even knocking at the door, they could be signaling unplanned developments and opportunities.

Reevaluate and Adjust Your Strategy

Well-run companies fine-tune their business strategies on a regular basis. They sell off or shut down products or business lines that are underperforming and develop or acquire new capabilities that keep them competitive. In other words, they constantly adapt to macro and industry changes. Doing so keeps them alive and vibrant.

One of the biggest surprises owners of midsize companies have is when they decide the time has come to sell, and they start thinking about a list of 5 or 10 buyers who have previously approached them with interest in their company. Some on the list will be from five years ago, others from the past year. The client believes this list is golden, but it usually is not. When contacted, those prospective buyers often say, "Oh, that was last year's strategy. We're no longer looking to acquire companies like that. Let me tell you what we're looking for now." Sometimes, strategies shift on a dime. Once, we were in negotiations with a blue chip company with great integrity. The company offered to buy a client's company and promised us the deal was solid and would close in two weeks. All it needed was the final approval of its parent company in Japan, which had approved every past acquisition. What happened next stunned the acquisition team. The strategy of the parent company had changed at the board level before it could be transmitted to the operating units. The deal was rejected. Strategies are a moving target and in many ways have to be.

Your strategy must be similarly dynamic and flexible, ready to change as the business environment and growth opportunities evolve. As we discussed in Chapter 7, having multiple lines of business only increases the likelihood that you will need to rethink your strategy as the fortunes and prospects of those units shift over time. Your value drivers, too, will shift up or down, just like small mutual funds. Each one needs to be monitored and adjusted with an eye toward preserving and improving its score. In any given year, some value drivers may fall off your list, to be replaced by new and more urgent concerns. This is a natural part of the QuickValue process, and it should directly inform your strategy.

Metrics Mavens Hones Its Strategy

Having passed on the offer from Martin, the Metrics Mavens team is determined to do whatever it can to help the company attain its full potential. The team members know they have a good company. They also know from their Value Driver Score that parts of their business could be improved. In past years, those sore spots had been largely overlooked as the team focused on better technology and higher sales. QuickValue has shown that bolstering other areas could increase the company's value by millions of dollars.

Thus far, strategic planning has not been on Metrics Mavens' radar. Sylvia knows strategy matters, but in the years since she founded the company, the product has been so hot and growth so organic that she and her team have gotten by on the intoxicating idea that the only strategy is more success—just keep driving ahead with what's working and let the chips fall where they may. But as the company has grown and added new managers, and as success has attracted increasingly tenacious competitors, winging it feels less and less like the right answer. With her valuation complete, Sylvia vows to make formal, strategic planning a yearly endeavor. For now, though, she and the rest of the team dive into creating mini plans based on their value drivers.

They focus first on the four that brought the lowest scores: leadership (which scored 4 out of 10), competition (5), pricing power (3), and customer experience (2). Competition and pricing power are vital and will get a close examination. But since the team has more direct control over leadership and customer experience, it decides to start there.

Glenn's frank assessment that customer service was his biggest headache as sales manager really hit home. Sylvia asks him to participate in a series of calls and meetings with the company's top customers. His presence helps turn what might otherwise be polite, somewhat awkward encounters into valuable sessions. These customers know Glenn, and they know he does not mince words, and soon the conversation is flowing freely. "Your technology is great," says one, "but when I have an issue and can't get anyone on the line, I want to pull my hair out. That's when I start bugging Glenn—just to feel like someone's listening." The sessions reveal some other frustrations—ones that not even Glenn was aware of. For example, he and Sylvia hear that once research studies are completed, it's taking Metrics Mavens longer than its competitors to provide analysis of the results.

Based on this feedback, Metrics Mavens embarks on a broad program to revamp customer service top to bottom. Its mini plan includes:

Goal: Improve customer service.

Objective: Respond to every client inquiry within 24 hours and resolve any issues within 48 hours.

Action Plan:

1. Hire two representatives to exclusively respond to customer inquiries.
2. Track every problem and report on how and when it is solved.
3. Hold meetings every month to assess what is working and what is not.

Now, about the leadership problem. This one cuts close to home for Sylvia. But the honesty her team showed when discussing leadership during the QuickValue analysis convinces her this is an area she needs to address quickly. Replacing herself as CEO isn't an option, but she does hire an executive coach to help develop her leadership skills. The sessions are enlightening. Qualities she thought demonstrated commitment and drive—burrowing in on research, sequestering herself in her office to ponder next steps— were too often seen by staff as aloofness. Many of the staff were reluctant or even afraid to approach her with problems or ideas. Much as it pains her to take time away from research, she commits to a specific number of hours each week to visit with various employees and departments.

Leadership extends beyond the CEO, of course. Sylvia knows at some point she will be moving on from Metrics Mavens. Having a strong, committed team in place will not only add value in the short term; it will give the company the best shot at carrying on successfully if and when she decides to sell. Toward that end, Sylvia decides to adjust her incentive system for key executives. Until now, she has paid bonuses based on EBITDA growth. But QuickValue has given her the means to reward them on increasing the company's value, not its annual profits. Though the two are related, value is the end game, she believes. And now she can track progress by measuring her value every year.

She decides on a two-tiered bonus system. An annual bonus will be paid on the increase in value from one year to the next. A second, longer-term bonus will be based on how much the company sells for above the $88 million offered by Martin S.

Sylvia believes this new incentive system will motivate her team to take the company's success personally, now and for years to come.

CHAPTER 10

Selling Your Company

Several years ago, I met Eric Gregg and Scott Hedrick, a pair of entrepreneurs from Raleigh, North Carolina. I liked them right away. They were bright, funny, optimistic, hardworking, and absolutely fearless. Starting with a bare idea in 2008, Eric and Scott had built their company into a fast-emerging producer of conferences—branded as Digital Summit—for the digital marketing industry. Like many successful entrepreneurs, as their company transitioned from a startup operation into a recognized player in the field, they were getting restless, looking to be rewarded for the value they had already created. When I met them in 2016, they had been approached by a potential buyer and felt ready to consider a sale. I agreed to advise them on the offer.

The first thing that jumped out was how rapidly the company was growing. Gregg and Hedrick expected to double their revenue and EBITDA in 2017 alone. With growth like that in the cards, they were unable to reach an agreement with the buyer, who was not willing to pay them now what their business might be worth in a year. So, the entrepreneurs decided to hold onto the business and use the time to make some improvements, firm up their long-term strategy, and potentially realize a much higher payday later on. I introduced them to Jim Zielinski, a senior advisor at Oaklins. As CFO of a successful media and events business, Zielinski had developed a track record for driving value creation, and he now consulted to entrepreneurs. He got to know Gregg and Hedrick, attended some of their conferences, and learned all he could about their business and their value drivers. Zielinski liked their unique business model, hosting day or day-and-a-half conferences in large cities across the United States. They were also developing a loyal base—conference attendees who could, perhaps, be monetized in other ways. The quality of their events was high, with impressive speakers and strong recommendations from attendees and sponsors. However, they had not yet reached the scale that would convince buyers the business was rock solid, and their profitability waned as they reinvested in the business.

Months later, Zielinski and the Digital Summit founders agreed on several objectives: improve their financial controls, expand the number of conferences, prepare individual income statements for each conference, increase profitability, and hire a full-time CFO.

Two years later, Gregg and Hedrick reached out to me again. They had implemented many of the improvements

Zielinski recommended. Their business was nicely profitable, and the future looked even more promising based on the exciting ideas they had for long-term growth. This time we took the company to market and had serious interest from a handful of buyers. The company was sold for a handsome price that was more than twice the offer they considered in 2016. Gregg and Hedrick were nicely rewarded for all their hard work.

Not every entrepreneurial story ends like that, of course. Yet a yearly valuation as described in this book can help smooth your journey to the end of the entrepreneurial rainbow: a profitable sale. When a prospective buyer approaches with an offer for your company, you will be able to move quickly beyond the "wow" factor and get down to solid details. If the price should be higher, you can walk the buyer through your latest valuation as the basis for your counterargument. You already know your value drivers, so you will be able to articulate them in discussions with investment bankers and buyers. And you know your weaknesses (the value drivers where you perform poorly), so you can explain why they're not as significant as a buyer might think, and the active steps you're already taking to improve them. You will also have a firm grasp on the value of your business relative to other companies in your industry. If you decide now is not the right time to sell, you will have a solid basis for identifying areas where concerted improvement could boost your value when you are ready to sell. Either way, you can move forward with confidence that you have made a sound decision.

In this chapter, we are going to review the ins and outs of a sale—what buyers are looking for, the tactics they will try to use when negotiating, and how QuickValue can help you level the playing field or even tip things in your direction. Ideally, when an offer comes in, you have already been using QuickValue every year for a number of years. If you have not used it before and you are approached by a buyer, that is OK, too. Like Sylvia and her Metrics Mavens team, you can use QuickValue to prepare, on deadline, an estimate of what your business is worth. But selling does not have to involve fielding unsolicited offers. Depending on your situation, at some point you may want to actively test the waters by putting your business on the market. We will discuss how to use your QuickValue results to help your investment banker prepare your company for sale and to find the right buyer at the right price. First, though, let's get into the mind of that mysterious figure at the other end of the deal—the typical buyer.

Understanding What Buyers Want

Nothing thrills a buyer more than coming across an attractive company whose owner has no idea of its value. A sophisticated buyer going up against an inexperienced seller reminds me of those college football games that perennial powers schedule against inferior opponents to chalk up a win on their way to a bowl appearance. While history records occasional upsets, most of these games end exactly as everyone expects them to. The powerhouse uses its superior skills and resources to overwhelm a shell-shocked opponent. Ken Collins, a former partner at Oaklins, once told me that back in his days as an operating executive, a favorite tactic among buyers acquiring businesses from naïve sellers was to take all the company's excess cash as part of the transaction. Of course, the rule of thumb among those in the know is that the available cash belongs to the seller.

If you are *not* in the know, you could be helping the buyer fund the acquisition with your own cash, inadvertently reducing the purchase price and multiple at your expense.

That does not make buyers bad people. They are hard-nosed pragmatists looking for every legitimate advantage in a competitive and risky field. And like anyone else, they want a bargain if they can get it. If a seller has not bothered to carefully assess the value of something he or she has spent years or decades building, so be it. In such cases, all or most of the negotiating leverage belongs to the buyer.

Among sellers, all this creates a certain amount of understandable anxiety. That is just human nature, regardless of what is for sale. When I was in my twenties, I found a complete six-volume set of Winston Churchill's *The Second World War* at an estate sale for $18. I wasn't looking for a bargain. As a history lover, I just wanted to read and own the books. Nor had I attempted to dicker on the price. I handed over the exact amount on the price tag. Yet I've never forgotten the look the woman ringing up the sale gave me, as though I were taking advantage of the estate. "You're probably buying this for a song," she said. Expand that sentiment to people selling an entire business that they have poured everything into, and you can see why so many owners simply assume they are getting taken to the cleaners.

You do not have to feel that way. You can walk into a negotiating room with a confident demeanor backed up by a set of documents and numbers. You may not come away with every penny you hoped for, but experienced buyers will know they are dealing with a serious counterpart.

Valuation, with a Deadline Looming

Without warning, an offer lands on your desk. A month ago, a buyer approached you out of the blue with interest in acquiring your company. You agreed to provide the buyer with financial information after he signed a nondisclosure agreement. Now, he has surprised you by making what appears to be a bona fide offer. The numbers seem impressive, but it has been years since your last formal valuation. The first thing to consider is your time window. Ideally, you have a few weeks in which to evaluate the offer and respond. If that's the case, go ahead and conduct your first full QuickValue analysis just as described in the preceding chapters. The timeline will be tight, and you and your team will need to give the process your full attention. But you should be able to get the results you need in time, especially if your financial statements are already in good order.

Unfortunately, smart buyers often refuse to give the gift of time, fearing that you'll use those extra days to shop the offer around to other potential suitors. So, you may get as little as one week to consider an offer, along with a stern warning that as soon as the deadline passes, the offer expires and disappears. Do not disregard that warning. Do not assume that if the buyer really, *really* likes you, a few extra days won't matter. The industry lingo should convince you that the buyer is not fooling around: When deadlines pass, offers are said to "explode."

At this crucial phase, seller missteps—whether accepting an offer too quickly or dithering as the deadline slips by—can result in disaster. Another mistake is dismissing unexpected offers out of hand. On one trip to Seattle, I asked the owner of a small business to meet for coffee on behalf of a client interested in acquiring several companies in her field. This Seattle business fit her parameters nicely, and we were prepared to offer $5 million. But we never got the chance. Though the owner agreed to have coffee, he declined even to hear the offer. He was 91 years old, he explained, and absolutely loved what he was doing. In fact, he was adding a new product line soon. As admirable as his entrepreneurial spirit and forward outlook were, less than a year later he passed away. His wife had no interest in the business and sold it to an employee for $150,000. Too many owners respond in a similar fashion, cutting off interested buyers with, "I'm not for sale, and that's it." This is a mistake. You should at least listen to what a buyer might be offering and why. If nothing else, you will gain valuable information about how the outside world views your company.

If a tight deadline prevents you from conducting a full QuickValue review, you can still gain some clarity about the offer and improve your negotiating position. But you will have to prioritize. Here's an emergency plan:

- **Step 1.** Examine your financial statements and make the add-backs to EBITDA that we discussed in Chapter 3.

- **Step 2.** Consider whether your statements are based on accrual or cash accounting. You will recall that accrual is the preferred method because almost all buyers use it. If you use cash accounting, you obviously will not have time to convert. But you can ask your accountants or finance team to estimate how EBITDA would change for accrual accounting. This at least can help in evaluating whether the offer is fair.

- **Step 3.** Go directly to preparing public company comparables, as described in Chapter 5. With your public comparables in hand, adjust them for the private company discount. This step will give you a range of multiples to compare with a buyer's offer. Note that this means skipping the value drivers assessment detailed in Chapter 4. That's not ideal, but this is an emergency situation.

- **Step 4.** Now you can apply your adjusted EBITDA to the range of multiples to see what the actual value range is. You will not have a precise number to put on your company because you have not taken all the necessary steps. But if this exercise shows your range to be $60 million–$80 million and the offer comes in at $50 million, you will know that is too low. Having a range to gauge an offer by is considerably better than making a guess.

If it turns out that the offer is not right and you are going to hold onto the company, use this experience as a wake-up call. You have already completed a chunk of the QuickValue assessment. Go back, determine your value drivers and Value Driver Score, and complete the full process. Make that the first of yearly valuations and take comfort in knowing that the next time a prospective buyer comes calling, you will be prepared.

Fielding an Offer Using an Up-to-Date QuickValue

If you regularly use QuickValue, you are in command of the information you need. You know the value of your company, how the value has changed over time, and how it compares with that of others in your industry. You also know how values in your industry are trending because you have tracked the median value over several years. Are industry valuations ascending or declining? Is your business bucking the trends or in alignment with them? You will already know the answers to these important questions before a buyer comes knocking.

Even on a tight deadline, you will have time to share your valuation with other potential buyers, giving you the chance to see how they might value your business before you have to decide whether to accept the original offer. If you are like most sellers, you will want to do precisely what buyers want to prevent you from doing—making sure you are not missing out on a better deal.

When you have QuickValue in hand, negotiations with a prospective buyer might go something like this:

> **Buyer:** I'd like to buy your company for $120 million. How does that sound?
>
> **You:** That sounds pretty good, but let me ask you a few questions. How did you come up with that price?
>
> **Buyer:** We based our offer on a multiple of 12x EBITDA.
>
> **You:** So you are assuming $10 million in EBITDA. Over what time period are you calculating EBITDA?
>
> **Buyer:** We are using your calendar year, which ended December 31.

You: Well, that explains why the EBITDA you are using is $1 million lower than what we are using. We're three months into the next year and should get credit for that. Are you giving us credit for the $1 million in add-backs to EBITDA?

Buyer: No, we need to better understand why those add-backs are reasonable.

You: OK, fair enough. We can come back to that. More importantly, we believe the EBITDA multiple of 12x is too low. In our examination, we came up with 14x. Can I share my analysis with you?

Your secret weapon using QuickValue is knowledge of your value drivers. You know which business characteristics most influence your value. Most sellers have never given this much thought. They have been focused on revenue and EBITDA, only giving cursory attention to what makes their businesses unique and valuable. Since you can articulate these characteristics, you have a big advantage when selling your company.

Buyers will have their own ideas of what makes your company attractive to them, but they do not know your business the way you do. If you can help them identify benefits they are not aware of, they may be willing to pay even more.

Actively Seeking a Buyer

Not every sale involves waiting for someone else to make an offer. Perhaps you have taken the company as far as you can and you are ready to let someone else take over. You have other entrepreneurial dreams to fulfill. You have reached a point in life where you are ready to ease your foot off the pedal. Whatever your reason, you may want to sell your company. And, naturally, you are looking for someone who will not only respect its traditions and treat employees well, but pay top dollar, too.

Putting your company up for sale requires the same attention to detail that you gave to building it. Owners often assume buyers will overlook defects and recognize the underlying qualities that make their company special. My Oaklins colleague Maarten Wolleswinkel in the Netherlands recalls one cost-obsessed owner whose headquarters featured worn, stained carpeting and mismatched chairs, dirty walls that hadn't been painted in 30 years, and a forest of weeds sprouting up through cracks in the visitors parking lot. What the owner saw as signs of thrift, Maarten knew buyers would interpret as neglect. After some tense haggling, the owner agreed to spend $50,000 for basic landscaping, fresh paint, and other improvements that helped drive a $50 million sale.

Here are five common mistakes sellers make that you can avoid:

1. **Failing to get advice.** Conducting your own valuation has given you a great understanding of what your company is worth and what a buyer should be willing to pay. You are armed and ready to go. Yet the complexities of the actual sales process are such that unless you have previous experience, you should have an advisor to help navigate. Below, we'll discuss working with seasoned experts who can help guide the sales process.

2. **Consulting the wrong advisor.** When you seek advice, be sure any candidate has experience not just selling companies, but selling companies in your industry. My partner and I learned the importance of industry knowledge the hard way when we started our investment bank 25 years ago. Hungry for business, we represented a potential buyer in the apparel industry, whose nuances were a complete mystery to us. The deal went nowhere. Below, we'll see how to put advisor candidates to the test.

3. **Negotiating sequentially.** Some sellers prefer to negotiate with one favored buyer at a time while putting others on hold. I believe one reason is that when sellers are not sure what the company is worth, it is comforting to negotiate with someone they think best understands their business. But your leverage as a seller comes in having multiple prospects negotiating simultaneously. Below we will help give you the confidence to pit one buyer against another and negotiate the best price and terms.

4. **Approaching too few buyers.** Inexperienced sellers believe their company will be so attractive to a few buyers that going beyond this small group is a waste of time. Far from it. Some buyers on your imagined "short list" will have their own problems and not be in a position to make acquisitions. Others may have changed their strategies and may no longer be interested in your industry. Or they will have recently completed an acquisition and are pausing before they make another. Cast a wide net.

5. **Approaching the wrong buyers.** Some sellers, paranoid about letting competitors know they are for sale, refuse to approach buyers who may be in a position to make the best offers. For the same reasons, they may decide to only approach buyers who are outside of their industry. Ignoring the best buyers can be a serious mistake.

Ideally, by the time you put your company up for sale, you will already have at least one and preferably several yearly valuations under your belt. First and foremost, you will be likely to go into the process with realistic expectations. If a QuickValue review shows your company to be worth considerably less than you had hoped, you may even decide to hold off on that planned sale until you have made some improvements, thus sparing you and the company the embarrassment of finding out in a more public way that it is not worth what you thought.

As you move closer to putting the company on the market, you will likely want to seek the help of investment bankers to guide you through the sale process (see mistake 1, above). As you interview candidates, ask them to conduct their own valuation of your business, including identifying your key value drivers. Do this before you share your latest QuickValue results. Their response will show you how well aligned the bankers are with you and how well they understand your business. Is their valuation consistent with yours? Can they identify the key characteristics of your business that give it its value? A good investment banker might identify value drivers you are not even aware of because of their knowledge of what buyers are seeking.

Once you have chosen an investment banker, share your latest QuickValue with her and explain in detail how you arrived at your conclusions and where your analysis differed from hers. It will help her understand your strengths and weaknesses. She can use this information to emphasize your key value drivers and downplay those that need improvement. Because your investment banker will never understand your business the way you do, giving her the QuickValue analysis allows her to position your company for sale in the best possible way.

You are likely to have some value drivers where you score poorly. This is not necessarily a negative. For example, if you have a weak sales force, this problem can be easily solved with the right buyer. Your investment banker will know which buyers already have strong sales forces that can replace or supplement your team. Instead of seeing a weak sales team as a detriment and deducting from your value, these buyers can easily overcome what might be a value-reducing problem for other buyers. When you know the worth of your business and the key value drivers, this knowledge puts you in the driver's seat for negotiations. Instead of reacting in a vacuum to offers from buyers, you can compare the offers with your QuickValue results and respond decisively.

Metrics Mavens' Ship Comes In

Three years have passed since Sylvia declined the acquisition offer by Martin S. She, Joanna, and the rest of the company have used that time wisely. Based on the findings of their first valuation, they've made some important changes.

The team's initial value driver assessment showed customer experience (value driver 31) scoring just 2 of 10 possible points, seriously lagging the quality of Metrics Mavens' products. A new customer response program actively reaches out to customers to gauge their happiness and ensures a human voice at the other end of the line, followed up by action, for those who have problems. Though the system still is not perfect, customer complaints have dropped to the point that the team feels comfortable scoring customer experience at 7 rather than 2.

These and other improvements have helped a good company become even better. Gone are the days when Sylvia wondered abstractly what her company was worth and whether the investments in new products and services were paying off. Though she is still enthusiastic about the company and her own role as owner and CEO, she often thinks back to the negotiations with Martin S., wondering how her life would have changed if he had been willing to meet her counteroffer. Two things are for sure: Metrics Mavens is worth even more now than it was back then, and the next time an offer comes her way, she will be ready with a response.

In those three years, Metrics Mavens' adjusted EBITDA has increased to $14.6 million. And in the most recent QuickValue assessment, the company's Value Driver Score stands at 76 percent, up from 66 percent three years before. The company has gained points in customer experience, just as planned. This is all good news, but there is more. During this time, the EBITDA range for market research companies had increased as well. The new range is an upper median of 15.1x and a lower median of 9.3x. When adjusted for the 20 percent private company discount, the range is 12.1x for the upper median to 7.4x for the lower median. Applying the higher Value Driver Score of 76 percent to the spread of 4.7x increases Metrics Mavens' EBITDA multiple to 11x (3.6x added to 7.4x) as compared with 9.3x from three years earlier.

Sylvia feels as though she has hit the trifecta. The company's adjusted EBITDA, Value Driver Score, and QuickValue multiple have all increased. When the team applies the 11x multiple against $14.6 million in EBITDA, the QuickValue is now $161 million. Sylvia can hardly believe her eyes. And to think she'd come close to selling her company for $88 million just three years earlier.

Sylvia has always heard that the best time to sell a business is when it is performing well. In three years, the company's Value Driver Score increased by 10 percentage points.

She calls Ken S., an investment banker with expertise in market research whom she has been speaking with informally for the past year or so. They discuss how much the business might be worth, who the likely buyers are, and how Ken might go about marketing the company for a sale. She asks him to prepare a detailed analysis. A week later, he comes back with an independent valuation based on his knowledge of industry multiples, of Metrics Mavens' reputation relative to the competition, and other information he has gathered. He thinks she will be thrilled with his results.

"Hold onto your armrests," he says. "There are no guarantees, but I think we could get as much as $150 million for your company."

"I think we're worth more," she responds without hesitation.

Ken inwardly cringes. Is Sylvia going to be one of *those* owners, so in love with their business they assume buyers will pay anything just for the privilege of owning it?

Then, Sylvia lays out her case. She bolsters her case with past years' reports, showing steady improvements and progress in key areas. The more she speaks, the more Ken comes around. Sylvia is not dreaming; she has solid facts and objective analysis driving her argument that Metrics Mavens is worth at least $10 million more than his estimation.

Ken recommends a two-stage auction process: initial bids followed by a second round where buyers will be given more detailed information and access to the management team. When the sale process starts, nearly 100 market research firms and private equity investors are contacted, and 50 express interest in Metrics Mavens. Over the next several weeks, prospective buyers ask detailed questions about the business and about Sylvia's personal intentions. Does she aim to sell and move on, or will she stay for a few years? Sylvia, never the born manager, is looking for a clean break from the company that she still loves, but that seems to involve too many management headaches and less time for hands-on innovation.

Of the initial 50 prospective buyers, 8 submit formal bids, ranging from above Sylvia's target sale price to well below it. Ken and Metrics Mavens invite four buyers into round two. Three are market research companies, and one is a private equity investor who was already working with a CEO-in-waiting. A bid from another private equity investor, while higher than the target, required Sylvia to stay with the company and so is rejected.

In the second round, buyers zero in on the company's future prospects for the business. The team's deep knowledge of value drivers, passed along to Ken, helps guide these conversations.

In the end, the private equity firm drops out to focus on a separate acquisition that looks more promising, but all three market research candidates come through with offers ranging from $160 million to $170 million. After additional rounds of negotiation, one buyer stands out. The winner not only comes through with an offer of $172 million ($11 million above the QuickValue assessment), but it is a perfect fit. The buyer's complementary services and high regard for Metrics Mavens hold out the promise that Joanna, Glenn, and the rest of the Metrics Mavens staff have solid futures with the new venture.

The deal serves as validation of the team's efforts to fully understand the company's value, of the decision to decline Martin's initial offer three years earlier, and of all the improvements the company has made since then. For Sylvia, this represents the culmination of a dream she had hardly dared entertain when she started her business from scratch. She is not sure what the future holds for her. Will she start thinking of her next entrepreneurial challenge, or will she catch the next ferry to Nantucket? Either way, she will move forward with good feelings and no regrets, knowing she made a sound deal for herself and for the people and company she cares about.

The Company You Are Now

Congratulations, you have done it. You have identified not just what your company is worth, but which underlying value drivers support that figure. You understand your company at a deeper level than before, and you have the tools in place to take it to the next level.

Stop to consider where you were before you had this knowledge—a great company, working hard every day to deliver the best products or services to your customers. You took just pride in what you had built. At the end of each year, you tallied revenue and EBITDA, and the signs were positive. You felt confident in your ability to keep your staff gainfully employed, create value, and one day hand the company down as a family legacy or reap the rewards of a profitable sale. Yet when the pressures of daily business gave you a moment to come up for air, there were some nagging questions. Did the EBITDA multiple tossed around at the last industry conference you attended really apply to your company? What was your plan for building on your strengths? Were you addressing weaknesses strategically or mainly reacting to emergencies? Was the "gut instinct" decision-making process still working, or did it sometimes feel like shooting in the dark? Maybe these were some of the things keeping you up at night.

Now consider where you are after investing a modest amount of time and energy in learning what is really driving the value of your business. From here on:

- Each year, you will build your strategic plan with a clear, methodical eye toward building value. And you will spend less time and resources on projects that are not producing value.

- If your company is involved in more than one business, you will know what each part is worth and can make decisions appropriate for each.

- You will have the means to reward and incentivize your key executives based on value creation rather than growth in revenue and EBITDA.

- When you seek funds for expansion, you will have a head start with lenders and investors and have a strong case to make about what your company is worth.

- If you receive a surprise offer for your business, you will know from the outset if the offer is in the right range.

- When the time comes to sell, you will have a detailed knowledge of your value, one that can put you on a more even footing with any potential buyer.

I hope that you have found the information and processes in this book useful and that you will make QuickValue part of your yearly routine. As you proceed on this journey, stay in touch! Look to www.quickvaluemethod.com for more resources and updates in the months and years to come. The future is yours.

Income Statement Adjustments

Revenue and EBITDA are the metrics used in valuations. You will find both on your income statement. In some cases, the last entry on your income statement will be "Net Income" instead of "EBITDA." If that is the case, you will need to make some adjustments to determine EBITDA. If your revenue or expenses include interest, or your expenses include taxes, depreciation, and amortization, these items need to be adjusted from net income to arrive at EBITDA. A quick reminder: The "ITDA" in "EBITDA" is "interest, taxes, depreciation, and amortization," and the "EB" is "earnings before." Interest income is subtracted from net income. Expenses for interest, taxes, depreciation, and amortization are added back.

Once you determine EBITDA, you may need to make further adjustments to remove owner perks and other extraordinary items. These items are aberrations from normal operations. Removing them will allow you to report "normalized" results as if the revenue and expenses associated with these items never occurred. Owner perks are expenses that are unrelated to the business and for the benefit of the owners. Other extraordinary items can be revenue and expenses and are either non-operating or non-recurring. Non-operating items are unnecessary to the business. Non-recurring items are infrequent or unusual and unlikely to happen again.

Table A.1 offers an example of the calculations that allow you to arrive at EBITDA and adjusted EBITDA.

In summary, the calculation of EBITDA is *after* interest, taxes, depreciation, and amortization, and the calculation of adjusted EBITDA is *after* owner perks and other extraordinary items. To create a normalized income statement that can be used in a valuation, you must remove these items: (1) interest, (2) taxes, (3) depreciation, (4) amortization, (5) owner perks, and (6) other extraordinary expenses.

Below is a checklist of revenue and expenses often found in owner perks and other extraordinary items:

Owner Perks

Owner perks include:

- Excess owner compensation
- Family members on the payroll
- Personal travel and entertainment

TABLE A.1 Sample Income Statement Adjustments

Income Statement ($)	
Revenue	
Sales	50
Interest income	2
Total Revenue	**52**
Expenses	
Salaries	10
Rent	10
Product costs	15
Interest expense	1
Taxes	5
Depreciation	2
Amortization	2
Total Expenses	**45**
Net Income	**7**
Adjustments to Net Income	
Interest income	(2)
Interest expense	1
Taxes	5
Depreciation	2
Amortization	2
Total Adjustments to Net Income	**8**
EBITDA	**15**
Adjustments to EBITDA	
Owner perks	1
Other extraordinary items	1
Total Adjustments to EBITDA	**2**
Adjusted EBITDA	**17**

- Personal tax preparation
- Personal items (cell phone, dry cleaning, flowers, etc.)
- Life insurance
- Automobiles, planes, yachts
- Car and home repairs
- Country club memberships
- Vacation home

Other Extraordinary Items

These include non-operating and non-recurring items.

Non-operating

Items that can show up as revenue or expenses and result in gains or losses:

- Investments, including dividends
- Sale of an asset (building, business line)
- Lawsuit judgment
- Currency exchanges
- Insurance claims
- Discontinued operations (closing a plant, discontinuing a product or business line)
- Above or below market rent

Items that can show up as expenses:

- Legal fees for a lawsuit

- Obsolete inventory

- Restructuring expenses such as severance

- Repairs from damages due to a natural disaster

- Excess rent payments for unoccupied space

- M&A fees (investment bankers, accountants, lawyers) for a sale or acquisition

Non-recurring

Typical non-recurring items are:

- Moving expenses for relocating offices

- Severance payments to former employees

- Cost of a new production system

- One-time repairs or renovations

If you have suggestions for owner perks or other extraordinary items, please suggest them at www.quickvaluemethod.com.

APPENDIX **2**

Resources for Finding Your Industry's Public and Private Multiples

- At www.quickvaluemethod.com, you will find a list of
  over 100 industries. For each, you will find the upper
  and lower medians for public companies. Also provided
  is the median, which can be compared with the median
  for private transactions, allowing you to determine
  the private company discount (this is the percentage
  difference between the multiples that public and private
  companies sell for). My colleagues at Oaklins have made
  these multiples available through an arrangement with
  S&P's Capital IQ.

Here is list of some of the 100 industries:

- Automotive OEM suppliers

- Building materials

- Cheese

- Digital media

- Distribution

- Energy infrastructure

- Enterprise SaaS

- Flexible packaging

- Food ingredients

- Glass processing and finishing

- Healthcare practitioners and clinics

- Horticulture

- Human resources

- HVAC

- Marine equipment

- Market research

- Online gambling

- Pet care

- Robotics

- For B2B SaaS companies, an excellent resource can be found at www.saas-capital.com. This site presents an updated median public company multiple at the end of each month. Because this industry's valuations are based on revenue, the multiple used is annualized run-rate revenue. Based on SaaS Capital's experience with 30 private companies, it estimates the private company discount to be 28 percent.

- Woodside Capital Partners (www.woodsidecap.com), an investment bank in Palo Alto, California, provides reports with multiples for these technology industries: software, hardware, health tech, and internet/digital media.

- Hyde Park Capital (www.hydeparkcapital.com), an investment bank in Tampa, Florida, produces quarterly reports on six broad industries, with further breakdowns for each: technology, business services, financial services, healthcare, industrial services, and consumer.

If you have a suggestion for where other industry multiples can be found, please let us know at www.quickvaluemethod.com.

Additional Resources

Books

- *Valuation: Measuring and Managing the Value of Companies* (7th ed.), by McKinsey & Company with Tim Koller, Marc Goedhart, and David Wessels, 2020. This book is described as the bestselling guide to corporate valuation. It weighs in at a hefty 878 pages and covers just about every topic related to valuation that you can imagine.

- *Investment Valuation: Tools and Techniques for Determining the Value of Any Asset* (3rd ed.), by Aswath Damodaran, 2012. This comprehensive (974-page) volume was written by a professor of finance at New York University's Leonard N. Stern School of Business.

- *The Market Approach to Valuing Businesses* (2nd ed.), by Shannon P. Pratt, 2005. This 389-page book is devoted to a single valuation method: the market approach.

- *Measure What Matters: How Google, Bono, and the Gates Foundation Rock the World with OKRs,* by John Doerr, 2018. John Doerr, one of the most successful venture capitalists, writes about some simple objectives to use for your planning.

- *Good Strategy Bad Strategy: The Difference and Why It Matters,* by Richard P. Rumelt, 2011.

- *Strategy That Works: How Winning Companies Close the Strategy-to-Execution Gap,* by Paul Leinwand and Cesare Mainardi, 2016. Recommended by Mark Leiter, former chief strategy officer of Nielsen.

- *Your Strategy Needs a Strategy: How to Choose and Execute the Right Approach,* by Martin Reeves, Knut Haanaes, and Janmejaya Sinha, 2015. Written by a global team at the Boston Consulting Group. Recommended by Mark Leiter.

- *Mergers & Acquisitions Playbook: Lessons from the Middle-Market Trenches,* by Mark Filippell, 2010. This is the best book I have come across about M&A for midsize companies. It was written by my Oaklins colleague Mark Filippell, a partner in our Cleveland office.

Websites

- Check in at www.quickvaluemethod.com for new and updated information relevant to QuickValue, including suggestions from readers.

- SaaS Capital created the SaaS Capital Index, which follows the valuation metrics for 64 public companies that are "pure-play, B2B SaaS businesses." Metrics are a multiple of annual run-rate revenue. SaaS Capital is based in the United States and invests in SaaS companies. Go to www.saas-capital.com.

- The Association for Corporate Growth aims to drive middle-market growth by serving 90,000 investors, owners, executives, lenders, and advisors to global middle-market growth companies. Go to www.acg.org.

- MCM Capital has a wealth of information on its website, under the tab "Education." Blogs, videos, and white papers (under the name "Well Capitalized") explain how private equity and valuation work. Go to www.mcmcapital.com.

White Papers

- *What's Your SaaS Company Worth?*, by Rob Belcher of SaaS Capital, 2019. This excellent 19-page report can be found at www.saas-capital.com.

If you have other ideas for resources, please suggest them at www.quickvaluemethod.com.

Notes

Chapter 1

1. Stewart, James B., *DisneyWar*, Simon & Schuster, 2005.
2. The National Center for the Middle Market.
3. "What's Your SaaS Company Worth?," White Paper by SaaS Capital, 2019.
4. As of 2017. Consultancy.org.

Chapter 2

1. *Valuation: Measuring and Managing the Value of Companies* (7th ed.), McKinsey & Company, with Tim Koller, Marc Goedhart, and David Wessels, 2020.

Chapter 3

1. A few industries prefer other measurements than EBITDA for valuations. For example, SaaS companies use annual recurring revenue, and television and cable companies use broadcast cash flow. If your industry uses something other than EBITDA, you can use that metric if the information you have about comparable multiples is also in that format.

Chapter 4

1. "Top 150 Global Licensors," License Global, 2020.
2. Ibid.

Chapter 5

1. Pratt, Shannon, *The Market Approach to Valuing Businesses*, 2nd ed., 2005, John Wiley & Sons.

Chapter 7

1. Walters, Natalie, "Who Knew? Netflix Still Has 2.7 Million DVD-by-Mail Subscribers," The Motley Fool, February 2, 2019.
2. "What's Your SaaS Company Worth?," White Paper by SaaS Capital, 2019.

Chapter 8

1. Various authors, "What Private Equity Has to Teach Public Companies," *Strategy&*, 2011.
2. National Center for the Middle Market, August 25, 2020.
3. Goldstein, Matthew, "Private Equity Firms Return to Piling on Debt to Pay Dividends," *New York Times*, February 20, 2021.

Chapter 9

1. Stoll, John D., "Technology Drives Deals Because No One Wants to Be the Next Blockbuster," *Wall Street Journal*, May 29, 2019.
2. Rana, Preetika, and Farrell, Maureen, "How Airbnb Pulled Back from the Brink," *Wall Street Journal*, October 12, 2020.

Index

Page numbers followed by *f* and *t* refer to figures and tables, respectively.

About the Authors

Reed Phillips is chairman of Oaklins International, one of the world's largest midmarket M&A organizations with 850+ investment bankers in 45 countries. His firm has completed transactions with Microsoft, TripAdvisor, *The New York Times*, Conde Nast, Oracle, Thomson Reuters, Deloitte, S&P Global, and Deutsche Börse. Phillips cofounded Oaklins DeSilva & Phillips, a specialty investment bank for the marketing, media, information, and technology industries, which has completed nearly 400 M&A transactions, financings, and valuations.

Before he became an investment banker, Phillips spent ten years as an entrepreneur and executive at midsize companies in the roles of founder, CEO, vice president, and associate publisher. He is a graduate of Duke University with an A.B. in Management Sciences and lives in Manhattan with his wife and two dogs.

Charles Slack is a business and financial writer and award-winning author of four books, including *Liberty's First Crisis: Adams, Jefferson, and the Misfits Who Saved Free Speech*, and *Hetty: The Genius and Madness of America's First Female Tycoon*. He is a graduate of Harvard and lives with his wife in Connecticut.